Section of Advent Window
Plymouth Congregational Church
Minneapolis, Minnesota
Designed by Henry Lee Willett

Volume forty-seven

Christmas

An American Annual of Christmas Literature and Art

Edited by Randolph E. Haugan

Augsburg Publishing House
Minneapolis

Table of Contents

Volume Forty-seven

First Edition

Nineteen Hundred Seventy-seven

Acknowledgments

SYMBOLISM IN STAINED GLASS 18-22
This article is excerpted from the book "Symbolism in Stone and Glass" by Howard J. Conn with his permission. All windows designed by Henry Lee Willett. Photography: Dean Paris.

A LITTLE TOWN WHOSE INDUSTRY WAS CHRISTMAS . . . 23-25
Copyright 1975 Smithsonian Institution, from SMITHSONIAN Magazine, December 1975. Photo: Ralph Crane.

CHRISTMAS IN LITTLE DENMARK 45-48
King Merrill Photos

CHRISTMAS MUSIC 53-60
Calligraphy by Hildegard Szendrey. Illustrations by Audrey Teeple.

GOOD KING WENCESLAS 52
Suggestion of using text of "Good King Wenceslas" carol with stamps made by Anne Delfeld.

SALZBURG'S CRÈCHE/TOY EXHIBIT 61-66
All photos credited to curator of Salzburg's museum, the Carolino Augusteum.

LAYOUT AND DESIGN: George Nordwall

MUSIC EDITOR: Allan Mahnke

EDITORIAL ASSISTANT: Melva Rorem

The Christmas Story

According to St. Luke and St. Matthew

Illustrations by Paul VanDemark

AND IT CAME TO PASS in those days, that there went out a decree from Caesar Augustus, that all the world should be taxed. (And this taxing was first made when Cyrenius was governor of Syria.) And all went to be taxed, every one into his own city. And Joseph also went up from Galilee, out of the city of Nazareth, into Judaea, unto the city of David, which is called Bethlehem; (because he was of the house and lineage of David:) To be taxed with Mary his espoused wife, being great with child. And so it was, that, while they were there, the days were accomplished that she should be delivered. And she brought forth her firstborn son, and wrapped him in swaddling clothes, and laid him in a manger; because there was no room for them in the inn. And there were in the same country shepherds abiding in the field, keeping watch over their flock by night. And, lo, the angel of the Lord came upon them, and the glory of the Lord shone round about them: and they were sore afraid.

AND THE ANGEL SAID unto them, Fear not: for, behold, I bring you good tidings of great joy, which shall be to all people. For unto you is born this day in the city of David a Saviour, which is Christ the Lord. And this shall be a sign unto you; Ye shall find the babe wrapped in swaddling clothes, lying in a manger. And suddenly there was with the angel a multitude of the heavenly host praising God, and saying, Glory to God in the highest, and on earth peace, good will toward men. And it came to pass, as the angels were gone away from them into heaven, the shepherds said one to another, Let us now go even unto Bethlehem, and see this thing which is come to pass, which the Lord hath made known unto us. And they came with haste, and found Mary, and Joseph, and the babe lying in a manger. And when they had seen it, they made known abroad the saying which was told them concerning this child. And all they that heard it wondered at those things which were told them by the shepherds. But Mary kept all these things, and pondered them in her heart. And the shepherds returned, glorifying and praising God for all the things that they had heard and seen, as it was told unto them.

NOW WHEN JESUS was born in Bethlehem of Judaea in the days of Herod the king, behold, there came wise men from the east to Jerusalem, saying, Where is he that is born King of the Jews? for we have seen his star in the east, and are come to worship him. When Herod the king had heard these things, he was troubled, and all Jerusalem with him. And when he had gathered all the chief priests and scribes of the people together, he demanded of them where Christ should be born. And they said unto him, In Bethlehem of Judaea: for thus it is written by the prophet, And thou Bethlehem, in the land of Juda, art not the least among the princes of Juda: for out of thee shall come a Governor, that shall rule my people Israel. Then Herod, when he had privily called the wise men, enquired of them diligently what time the star appeared. And he sent them to Bethlehem, and said, Go and search diligently for the young child; and when ye have found him, bring me word again, that I may come and worship him also. When they had heard the king, they departed; and, lo, the star, which they saw in the east, went before them, till it came and stood over where the young child was. When they saw the star, they rejoiced with exceeding great joy. And when they were come into the house, they saw the young child with Mary his mother, and fell down, and worshipped him: and when they had opened their treasures, they presented unto him gifts; gold, and frankincense, and myrrh. And being warned of God in a dream that they should not return to Herod, they departed into their own country another way.

AND WHEN THEY WERE departed, behold, the angel of the Lord appeareth to Joseph in a dream, saying, Arise, and take the young child and his mother, and flee into Egypt, and be thou there until I bring thee word: for Herod will seek the young child to destroy him. When he arose, he took the young child and his mother by night, and departed into Egypt: And was there until the death of Herod: that it might be fulfilled which was spoken of the Lord by the prophet, saying, Out of Egypt have I called my son. . . . But when Herod was dead, behold, an angel of the Lord appeareth in a dream to Joseph in Egypt, saying, Arise, and take the young child and his mother, and go into the land of Israel: for they are dead which sought the young child's life. And he arose, and took the young child and his mother, and came into the land of Israel.

Mary, Mother of Jesus

ALVIN N. ROGNESS

The Annunciation
Richard Heule

A baby is the central figure of the Christmas drama. The others are supporting players at best. The angelic hosts, the adoring shepherds, the Wise Men from the east, King Herod—all are incidental to the drama. It is the baby Jesus who is the light of the world.

Even the virgin mother has a brief assignment in the spotlight of the overwhelming incarnation event, God becoming man.

That night in Bethlehem had been foretold for centuries. In the wake of man's disobedience and estrangement, God had promised a savior. Again and again, through the prophets, the promise had been repeated. Then, in the fulness of time, God moved to fulfill his promise.

It was in the house of Zacharias that God first let it be known that the time had arrived. An angel came and announced ". . . your wife Elizabeth will bear you a son, and you shall call his name John . . . and he will . . . make ready for the Lord a people prepared."

Then the angel appeared again, this time to Elizabeth's cousin, Mary, a peasant girl in Nazareth, engaged to Joseph, a carpenter. She too was to bear a son, not by Joseph or by any man, but by the Holy Spirit. Something utterly new was to occur on earth. God was to become man, born of woman. The long promised Messiah would begin his advent in the womb of a virgin.

To Mary's incredulous question, "How shall this be, since I have no husband?" the angel replied:

> Do not be afraid, Mary, for you have found favor with God . . . The Holy Spirit will come upon you, and the power of the Most High will overshadow you; therefore the child to be born will be called holy, the Son of God.

Familiar as Mary may have been with some of the prophecies concerning a coming Messiah, the news brought by the angel must have left her bewildered and overcome. Had she been other than a girl of simple and uncomplicated devotion, she might have dismissed the whole event as illusion or nonsense. When a short time later she visited her cousin Elizabeth and told of the strange visit of the angel, Elizabeth, filled with the Holy Spirit, exclaimed, "Blessed are you among women, and blessed is the fruit of your womb!" From the lips of Mary we then have the words of the *Magnificat*, one of the most rhapsodic affirmations of faith and obedience in all the literature of the world.

And Mary said:

13

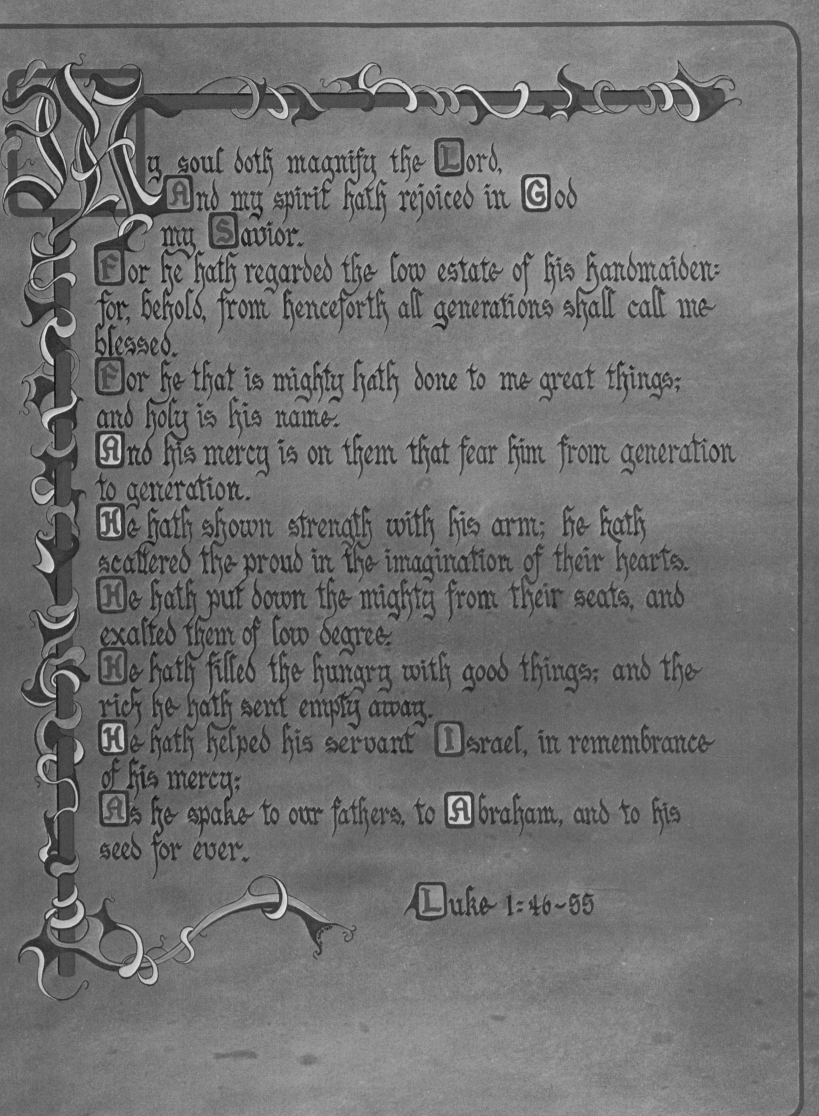

My soul doth magnify the Lord,
And my spirit hath rejoiced in God
my Savior.
For he hath regarded the low estate of his handmaiden: for, behold, from henceforth all generations shall call me blessed.
For he that is mighty hath done to me great things; and holy is his name.
And his mercy is on them that fear him from generation to generation.
He hath shown strength with his arm; he hath scattered the proud in the imagination of their hearts.
He hath put down the mighty from their seats, and exalted them of low degree.
He hath filled the hungry with good things; and the rich he hath sent empty away.
He hath helped his servant Israel, in remembrance of his mercy;
As he spake to our fathers, to Abraham, and to his seed for ever.

Luke 1: 46-55

She stayed with her cousin for three months. Joseph, meanwhile, had been reassured by the angel of God's intervention in the life of his betrothed.

Their lives in Nazareth were interrupted by a decree from the emperor, Caesar Augustus, who ordered a world-wide census—each family reporting to the village from which their ancestors had come. Because they were of the family of King David, Joseph and Mary had to go south to Judea and Bethlehem.

> And while they were there, the time came for her to be delivered. And she gave birth to her first-born son and wrapped him in swaddling cloths, and laid him in a manger, because there was no place for them in the inn.

The extraordinary events of the next hours and days filled them with awe and wonder. On the eighth day, when in observing the law of their faith they brought Jesus to the temple, they heard Simeon's cryptic prayer, "Lord, now lettest thou thy servant depart in peace, according to thy word; for mine eyes have seen thy salvation which thou hast prepared in the presence of all peoples."

Upon their return to Nazareth from their hurried flight to Egypt, nothing much is recorded either of Jesus or Mary (except for a pilgrimage to Jerusalem when the boy was 12) until he began his public ministry 30 years later. In the ensuing three years, Mary is virtually absorbed into the crowd of people that trailed Jesus in Galilee and Judea. It was as if the career God had chosen for Mary had ended.

But her name lives on. It is a name given by devout parents of all churches, and by parents not so devout, to more girls than any other in the western world. From queens and princesses to daughters of the humblest, the name of Mary is cherished as none other. And why not? Mary was the chosen. She was the mother of Jesus, of God the Son, of the Savior of the world.

The homage given to Mary of Nazareth has not been universal in the life of the Christian church, however. Within the Roman Catholic Church hundreds of cathedrals, shrines, and monastic orders carry her name. Music and art are lavish in her praise. The church is rich in prayers and liturgies in her honor. The request for her intercessions, "Mary, mother of God, pray for us," is on the lips of devout believers. In contrast, most of Protestantism appears to overlook Mary. Few chapels or churches bear her name. There are no prayers and few hymns for her. No institutions or orders commemorate her. It is almost as if there is a calculated plot to forget her.

What is known as the Marian movement, or Mariolotry, has a long history in the Roman Catholic Church, and constitutes an uneasy issue in the current effort for unity between the Protestant and Roman churches. The movement has a tradition all its own. The tradition, seldom anchored explicitly in Scripture, is considered by many Protestant scholars and not a few Catholic scholars as deflecting the central message of the gospel.

The Marian movement has its roots deep in the past. It developed in stages, originally as simple Christian piety reaching out toward the Virgin Mary. The Council of Ephesus (411 A.D.) was responsible for some liturgical formulations for Mary. Until the eighth century, the movement was found more in the East than in the Latin West, but by the 12th century it began to flower in Europe.

Although the *Doctrine of the Immaculate Conception* did not become dogma until 1854 when Pope Pius IX declared officially that ". . . the most blessed Virgin Mary was in the first instant of her conception . . . preserved free from every stain of original sin . . . ," already at the time of the Reformation the teaching was widely held. Even the *Doctrine of the Assumption* (the belief that Mary went to heaven without the benefit of death), although not made a dogma of the church until 1950 by Pope Pius XII, was also in the 16th century an integral part of the church's worship life.

It is not surprising that the reformers, with the renewed emphasis on the Scriptures as the only sure guide for the church's faith and life *(sola scriptura)*, should regard the adoration of Mary with suspicion. There was no evidence in the Bible text that Mary ascended to heaven without dying. And far from regarding herself without sin, she called God her Savior (Luke 1:47), thereby including herself among all mankind needing salvation.

It was not so much the homage paid to Mary that alarmed the reformers. The subtle but real reverence paid to the virgin as cooperating with her Son in the salvation of the world—with the further implication that not only Mary, but we too, could provide merits that would contribute to our salvation—caused them to re-evaluate the movement.

Among the reformers, Luther especially was fond of cherishing the memory of Mary. He said, "It is true, Mary is praiseworthy and can never be lauded and extolled enough. For the honor of having been chosen from all the women on earth to be the mother of this infant is exceedingly high and glorious . . . but the praise of the mother should be as a drop; the praise

15

The Magnificat
calligraphy by Mary King

Litho. in U.S.A.

of this infant should be as the entire expanse of the wide sea" (Weimar, Vol. 34, 500).

Neither did he object to her being called the Queen of Heaven, but cautioned that this "does not make her a goddess who could grant gifts or render aid, as some suppose when they pray and flee to her rather than to God. She gives nothing; God gives all" (Weimar, Vol. 7, 572 f). If all is by grace (sola gratia) through faith (sola fide), and this through the merits of Jesus Christ alone by the Spirit, then Mary, however honored, must take her place with all the men and women of the world for salvation. Whatever titles are given to Mary—Queen of Heaven, Mother of the Church, the second Eve, Co-redemptrix—other than "mother of Jesus," they find no support in Scripture.

In his book, *The Question of Mary*, Rene Laurentin, a distinguished Roman Catholic scholar in France, describes the situation in the 16th century. "The Protestant crisis occurred in a time of decadence. . . . Devotion to the Virgin Mary had been made insipid by sentimentality, had been corrupted by superstitious infiltrations, and rendered ridiculous by the inventions of credulity (collections of false miracles and vain promises of cheap salvation). It was the time of coy, simpering virgins, and generally of an art which, having lost the sense of the sacred, made of the Virgin Mary nothing more than a naturally beautiful woman. . . . These abuses stirred up the anti-Marian reaction of the reformers." Laurentin believes that if it had not been for these abuses, the reformers might have led Protestantism into a climate of devotion to the virgin, in spite of the opposition which grew out of the logic of their principle of justification by faith.

As the reformers began to focus on a wide assortment of abuses in the church, it was inevitable that extreme positions were taken on both sides of controversy. By 1523 Luther was led to say, "I desire that the cult of Mary be totally abandoned solely because of the abuses which arise from it" (Weimar, Vol. 10, 61). Laurentin points out that in response "The devotees of Mary are roused to indignation . . . which lends a kind of support to the very abuses which all should be trying to outgrow. So the two processes stir each other up and lead towards open conflict."

It is not difficult to understand how excessive sentiment for Mary could arise. Motherhood itself is associated with understanding, tenderness, and care; not always attributed to fathers, sons, or brothers. Nor is it strange that a distinguished son should have his honors spill over upon his mother. In fact, to push the mother aside and not attribute the son's qualities to her, in some measure at least, would seem cruel. In medieval Europe, the rise of chivalry which ennobled womanhood, added enthusiasm for the adoration of the virgin.

The reformers, on the other hand, seeking to minimize the Marian movement, could point to the Scriptures for evidence that Jesus had not gone out of his way to exalt his mother. Except for the nativity story, the four gospel writers scarcely mention Mary, and in instances where she does appear, it is as if Jesus almost disclaims her. When he was told that his mother and brothers were waiting for him, he said, "Who are my mother and my brothers?" Looking about him at the crowd, he continued, "Here are my mother and my brothers. Whoever does the will of God is my brother, and sister, and mother" (Mark 3:34b, 35). It is a bit absurd, of course, to conclude from this curt reply that Jesus did not have a deep affection for his mother. The scene at the cross, where he addresses John, "Behold, your mother!" certainly speaks his great love for her. After the resurrection the Scriptures mention Mary only one other time; she was with Jesus' followers in the Upper Room at prayer.

If Roman Catholics have given Mary too big a place in their life of worship, Protestants have probably been too cautious in giving her honor. Protestant churches are named St. Paul's, St. John's, St. Andrew's. If a church sign should be found to read, *St. Mary's Methodist Church*, most Protestants would be baffled.

There is nothing wrong for the church to remember with thanksgiving those people who have been chosen by God for special services, and in honoring them: Noah, Abraham, Moses, John the Baptist, the apostles, Augustine, St. Francis, St. Teresa, Luther, Calvin, John Wesley, Florence Nightingale — and Mary of Nazareth.

It is not necessarily wrong to surround their memories with legends, a mixture of truth and imagination born of affection, as long as the Lord is not robbed of his glory. We indeed glorify God by fruits of the Spirit blossoming in the lives of his people. The virtues of a Paul or a Wesley or a Mary may become a bit exaggerated as the generations recall with appreciation that the grace of God worked mightily within them.

The Lord in his heavens must smile at seeing his children become disturbed, and even divided, over giving honor or not giving honor to one another. We are all his children, equally in need of his grace, equally loved by him, destined to a non-hierarchical life with him forever. If there are ranks to be given, he has but one rule—the humble shall be exalted— and by that rule Mary may well be among the elite. The only qualification she has to commend her is that God made her unique by choosing her to be the mother of his Son, and this by grace alone. And are we not all chosen to be his own? As such, Mary can well be the symbol for us all.

Madonna and Child
Trygve M. Davidsen

The poet John Davidson wrote, "Love built this shrine. . . ." It was love indeed that built the chapel at Plymouth Congregational Church, Minneapolis, Minnesota: love for God, love for "seclusion from the hurrying throng," love that depicts the symbols of the church through the ages, love that desires for all who worship there the waiting Father's blessing.

It is the dream of Dr. Howard J. Conn, pastor there from 1944 to 1976, who tells its story here. And his dream encompasses in its stained glass windows every scene, every symbol, every text, and every religious concept— all brought wonderfully to life as they were transformed into creations of artistic beauty by Henry Lee Willett.

Each window is a sparkling marvel of color and light, and the celebration of the church year that each window depicts is told in luminous beauty. If you have in you any poetry, any feeling for the mystic loveliness of color and light, you will respond to the jeweled revelations here of the Gospel story. Some windows are like a single, gentle song. Others are like a mighty hallelujah, like a great choir with every voice uplifted in a hymn of praise.

They should be seen again and again. For fine stained glass seems to have movement and life that changes as the light changes—from dawn to dusk, from the subdued light of a gray day to drenching, golden sunlight, from May to October to December.

"Love built this shrine. . . ." And those who enter and linger here may find in words and scenes and symbols not only the subtle blending of form and light and color, but a fresh, transforming revelation of the Child of Bethlehem.

—MELVA ROREM

Stained Glass

HOWARD J. CONN

Windows by Henry Lee Willett

You enter the chapel at Plymouth Congregational Church through red leather doors. Looking up the red-carpeted aisle, you see the communion table, the hanging cross, the reredos canopy, and the beautiful blues and reds of the glass above. The heavy trusses and panels of the ceiling reach up in mysterious shadows that catch the feeling of the ancient Gothic.

When our chapel was planned, there was vision to see that no one factor could contribute more to the satisfying effect of the whole building program than a complete set of stained glass windows. A commission was given Henry Lee Willett of Philadelphia, one of the great artist-craftsmen of our time, to make the finest windows possible. He was reared in the best of medieval tradition, for his father and mother before him were outstanding workers in stained glass.

Willett is an artist with an intuitive sense for design and color, and one who is painstaking as to details. Much of his tracery design shows the influence of the pure Gothic. In the Plymouth Chapel he has given us a distinguished set of glass which conveys at its best the true spirit of life and color.

Of all the windows in Plymouth Church, the stained glass found in the chapel windows comes nearest to medieval glass of European cathedrals. Here are no fields of opalescent whiteness; the entire openings being filled with jewel-like glass of many colors. Hundreds of tiny pieces are leaded together in intricate patterns to fashion windows of rare beauty.

Modern practitioners of the stained glass art have gone back to the 12th and 13th centuries. The artists of that day executed the finest windows the world has ever seen. Using pot metal glass and mastering the subtleties of color, they created glory which has withstood the test of time. They sensed that the first function of glass is to introduce light and color rather than to carry a picture. Henry Adams, in his classic description of the Cathedral at Chartres, wrote: "No doubt the first command of the Queen of Heaven was for light, but the second, at least equally imperative, was for color."

As the sunlight waxes and wanes through a given day, there is an ever-changing pattern of tones and hues. The beauty of a window lies in this living movement in light.

The second function of medieval glass was to be instructive. In those days the printing press had not been invented. The mass of people had no books. In the windows of the cathedrals there came to be placed the great heroes of faith and other characters of biblical history. A worshipper could see in the glass scenes which reminded him of the teachings of our Lord. The scenes were not graphic likenesses of events; they were only symbols or stylized treatments. It was not intended that the worshippers look at a detailed naturalistic picture, but only that the medallion should call to mind from earlier days a story long familiar in their religious heritage.

We who are novices in the field of iconography often look at a medieval window without comprehending what is portrayed. Yet, as we study the details and become familiar with symbolism, we find the glass filled with rich teachings.

The chapel windows feature observances of the Christian year which go back to the earliest days of the church. Christmas and Easter early came to be recognized as focal points within the Christian year, for they celebrate the birth and resurrection of our Lord. Gradually other days gained significance, many of them being chosen because of their relationship to corresponding Jewish holy days.

The Christian year traditionally starts with Advent, beginning with the Sunday nearest November 30th, covering a period which always includes four Sundays, and ending with Christmas Eve.

It is a time of preparation for the coming of the Christ child. By some it has been referred to as "winter Lent," because it suggests the need for soul-searching and religious instruction if we are fully to appreciate the birth of Christ. Just as the ancient world waited for many centuries for the coming of the Messiah, so we prepare with anticipation for the recurrent coming of our Lord. The Christ child is born anew each year in the hearts of those who by earnest preparation make Christmas something more than a secular occasion.

Dom Cabrol caught the spirit of this season when he wrote:

"It is the near approach of the Son of God in the flesh for which one must prepare oneself with greater watchfulness and by the practice of works of charity: it is the voice of the prophets announcing the Messiah who comes: it is the world awaiting its Redeemer, sighing as the parched ground for the dew of heaven: it is St. Paul exhorting the faithful, awakening them from their sleep upon the vigil of the coming of Christ: it is John the Baptist, the last of the long line of prophets, who cries in the wilderness, 'Prepare ye the way of the Lord.'"

In the lovely Advent window the artist seeks to catch these overtones.

Around the border of this and its companion lancet "Christmas," three tokens of the season are effectively repeated: the holly, the candle, and the fir tree. The decorative balls on the trees have been etched out of "flash glass" to shine with a jewel-like radiance.

At the top is the annunciation to Mary. The archangel Gabriel, carrying the symbolic lily, kneels before Mary to tell her that she has found favor with God, and shall bring forth a son who shall be called "Jesus." The spirit of Mary is conveyed by the words of the *Magnificat*, "My soul doth magnify the Lord" (Luke 1:46-55).

The central figure is that of John the Baptist, the immediate forerunner of Jesus. Clothed in camel's hair, he lived in the desert subsisting on locusts and wild honey. He was the last of the long line of prophetic voices crying from the wilderness, "Prepare ye the way of the Lord" (Mark 1:1-9). We see him with hands uplifted in exhortation, his staff at his feet, and with the symbolic waters of the river Jordan beneath the rock on which he stands. Surrounding him are attentive listeners: young and old, rich and poor, and even a Roman soldier.

The lower panel of each lancet has been designed to suggest the contemporary significance of the particular season. Here we see a family making preparation for Christmas, a little tot helping her father trim the tree, while a boy and girl watch the mother prepare the traditional crèche. We may be sure that the mother is speaking to her children of the deeper meanings of this annual custom which brings such delight to childhood.

In ten tiny insert medallions, each only five inches in diameter, the artist has placed symbols relating to this particular season, thus greatly enriching the significance of the window as a whole.

The left-hand insert of the top panel contains the lily, symbolic of the virginity of Mary. It stands for purity whenever it is portrayed in Christian art. To the right is the symbol of Isaiah—a saw, which is the instrument of his reputed martyrdom. It is in Isaiah that we find the beautiful prophecies which tradition has come to associate with Jesus. In the ninth chapter are found the words so beloved: "For unto us a child is born, unto us a son is given; and the government shall be upon his shoulder. . . ."

At the left top of the middle section is the Jesse Tree, one of the celebrated symbols which memorialize the Davidic descent of Christ: "And there shall come forth a rod out of the stem of Jesse, and a branch shall grow out of his roots" (Isaiah 11:1). The Tree of Jesse window at Chartres Cathedral is probably the best known and most prized window in all stained glass.

To the right is the rose, symbolic of the messianic promise, "The desert shall rejoice, and blossom as the

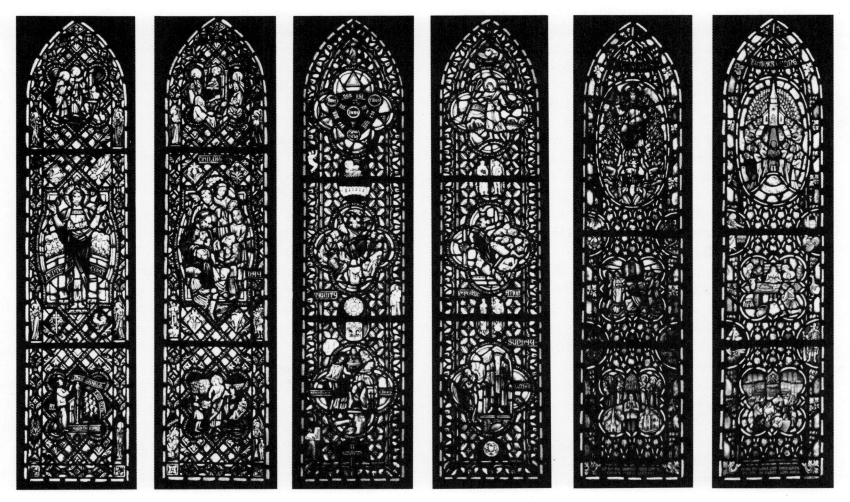

rose" (Isaiah 35:1). This symbol is also found frequently in Hebrew synagogues.

In the lower portion of this center section are two symbols of John the Baptist, to identify him as the figure above: the camel's hair coat and the nimbed Lamb standing upon a book and carrying the banner of victory because John the Baptist pointed to Jesus Christ, the Lamb of God.

Two appropriate forms of the cross are beautifully etched in the upper portion of the lower section. The Maltese cross on the left is sometimes called the regeneration cross, and is a symbol of the new birth for which we prepare at Advent. The eight outer points of this cross must be equidistant from one another, and are sometimes considered symbolic of the eight Beatitudes. The second, the Tau cross is a Latin cross without an upper arm. It is known as the Old Testament cross, or anticipatory cross, and as such is considered the Advent cross.

At the bottom are two candles burning in the night as signs of promise. On the right sits the watchman in the tower awaiting the first signs of morning light. "Watchman, what of the night?" (Isaiah 21:6, 11).

The Christmas window commemorates the birth of Jesus during Christmastide, which lasts from Christmas Eve until Epiphany, January 6th. The name "Christmas" was not used until the 12th century. It is a corruption of the term "Christ's Mass."

The selection of the date for Christmas illustrates the way in which our Christian festivals are related in origin to pagan or Jewish holidays. In the Julian calendar the winter solstice was mistakenly calculated at December 25. The Romans held elaborate games and winter celebrations at that time. The Christians found it convenient to compete with the pagans by establishing Christ's Mass at the same time. Just as the Romans gave presents at the winter festival, so the Christians adopted the same practice but related it to the gift of the Christ child. With the passing of the centuries and the spread of Christmas, celebrations of various lands were added to the observance, so that Christmas around the world is partly a folk festival as well as a holy day.

Christians ought always to recall the religious aspects of this season. It matters not what the actual date may have been; the birth of our Lord Jesus Christ is an event of supreme significance in world history.

In the upper section of the Christmas window is depicted the message of the angel to the shepherds. Three men kneel with folded hands. Even the lambs look up to hear the song of "peace on earth" (Luke 2:8-15).

In the center panel is the nativity scene, set in a crude manger with thatched roof. The oxen, the donkey, and a sheep all watch the holy family. Joseph stands above the madonna and child, holding in his right hand the lilies which according to an apocryphal tradition, bloomed from his staff when the group of prospects was gathered from whom the husband of the Virgin was to be selected. This is the legendary fulfillment of the prophecy contained in Isaiah 11:1.

Since Christmas is a time when we find special joy in doing things for others, the lower panel suggests as a modern application the spreading of cheer in a hospital ward. The artist pictures the figure in the nearest bed with a fever-flushed face, while the occupant of the far bed has the white face of approaching death. The children have brought a small tree and white gifts to the ward.

The ten small medallion inserts are of interest. At the top are portrayed the flight into Egypt (Matthew 2:13-15) and the innkeeper announcing that he has no room (Luke 2:7). Above the holy family, to the left, is the unicorn, that fabled animal whose mixed nature became symbolic of the incarnation. To the right is the Christmas rose, symbol of the nativity. Beneath the holy family, to the left, is the gladiolus, another and somewhat less common symbol of the incarnation, the Word made flesh. To the right is the daisy, in this conventionalized form symbolic of the innocence of the holy child.

The upper left medallion in the lower panel shows the poinsettia, a modern flower which we associate with the Christmas season. The upper right insert contains the fleur-de-lis, symbol of the Virgin Mary, or of the human nature of our Lord, or of the Trinity.

The lower two inserts suggest the folklore of Christmas. On the left the yule log is brought in. This Scandinavian custom held that the Christmas season lasts as long as the log burns, so the largest possible log is obtained. The hatreds and mistrusts of the past year are presumably consumed in its flame. On the right is Tiny Tim carried on the shoulders of Bob Cratchit, Dickens' beloved characters in A Christmas Carol. We can almost hear the familiar words, "God bless us, every one."

Symbolism in stained glass. . . . Symbolism that tells of the life and death and resurrection of our Lord. . . . Symbolism that speaks of light and color. . . . Symbolism that helps to lead the earthbound soul up to the very gates of heaven. The words of John of Damascus in the eighth century suggest the value of stained glass:

> I am too poor to possess books;
> I have no leisure for reading.
> I enter the church choked with the cares
> of the world; the glowing colors
> attract my sight like a flowering meadow,
> and the glory of God steals
> into my soul.

The village of Lauscha nestles in the Thuringians, now in East Germany.

A Little Town Whose Industry Was Christmas

PHILLIP SNYDER

SIXTY miles north of Nuremberg, Germany, high in the Thuringian mountains, deep in a forest of 80-foot-tall Christmas trees, sits the village of Lauscha. Its ornamentally decorated, slate-covered houses perch on steep streets nestled at the bottom of a narrow mountain valley. In the 1930s Lauscha looked like a storybook German town.

At that time most of the glass ornaments on American Christmas trees came from the immediate vicinity of this little town. Lauscha was the birthplace, in the 1840s, of a cottage industry that supplied virtually all blown glass Christmas tree ornaments until just before World War I, when a Viennese company began to copy the Lauscha ornaments. Later, Polish and Czechoslovakian glassblowers did the same, but Lauscha remained the principal ornament-maker for the United States up to World War II.

By 1930, approximately 2000 homes and 6000 people in the immediate vicinity of the hamlet were engaged in a craft almost unchanged since before the turn of the century. An ornament-maker's home was his factory. His wife and family were its staff and assembly line.

If you dropped in on a glassblower unexpectedly, you would probably find him perched on a high stool, bent over his bench, clad only in his long underwear, a pair of brown leather slippers on his feet. Behind him, far from the flame of a gas burner, were drums of lacquer and a hot pot of silvering solution, a combination of silver nitrate, quicklime, and milk sugar. Every glassblower had his own family formula.

His wife handled the tedious job of silvering the inside of the ornaments. She filled each one-quarter full with the solution, then shook it. To keep the silvering spreading evenly, she dipped the bulb in hot water several times. Uneven silvering showed through even after the ornament had been lacquered, and wholesalers would turn those ornaments down. After the coating was complete, she poured the excess solution into a basin where the silver was chemically sep-

23

arated to be used again. Then she hung the ornaments up to dry in rows from the ceiling rafters.

The following morning most of the silvered ornaments were dipped in various colored lacquers. The family grew so accustomed to the overpowering smell of lacquer that they scarcely noticed it, but others never got used to it. An importer who visited the village in the 1930s said that as you approached in a car, you could tell while still 100 feet away that you'd come to a glassblower's cottage.

All members of the family helped with the painted trimming that decorated many of the ornaments. When the paint was dry, the oldest child was entrusted with scoring the six-inch stems or "pikes" with a small blade coated with an abrasive. Once scored, the pike broke off easily and cleanly. Then the youngest child was given the job of fitting on little metal caps. Working 8 to 15 hours, a family could make from 300 to 600 ornaments a day, often six days a week.

Glassmaking began in Lauscha in the 1590s when religious persecution in the German province of Swabia forced groups of Protestant glassmakers to leave their homes. They were drawn to the Thuringian mountains by an abundance of wood, sand, and limestone, the necessary ingredients for glassmaking. In 1597, with the help of the Duke of Coburg, they built a small glass factory in Lauscha.

Gradually, the village became a center for drinking glasses, bull's-eye window glass, and other products which were sold by peddlers. But as more glassmakers were drawn to this center, authorities decided to limit new factories because of the heavy demand they were making on the wood supply from local forests. As a result, some glassblowers set up home workshops.

In the middle of the 18th century some of these craftsmen began to make glass beads, supplying jewelry and millinery trades throughout Europe. But glassblowers in Bohemia developed a method of making shinier beads than those produced in Lauscha, and almost overnight Lauscha lost most of its bead market. Hard times prevailed until a Lauscha glassmaker succeeded in duplicating the Bohemian's silvering formula. He saved the remnant of the town's business.

He also blew thick-walled glass balls which he silvered with his new mirroring solution. Since the 1820s heavy glass balls had been made by Lauscha craftsmen experimenting to see how large a bubble they could blow. They were known as *Kugeln* and many had been "silvered" inside with lead or zinc to make them reflect. Some were fastened to wooden crowns and hung from the ceiling during the Christmas season. The first written record of glass Christmas tree balls being produced was in 1848, when "six dozen of Christmas tree ornaments in three sizes" were recorded by a Lauscha glassblower.

In 1867 a gasworks was built in Lauscha. For the first time glassblowers had a steady, very hot, easily adjustable flame, making possible large, thin-walled bubbles of glass. A paper-thin one-inch version of the old heavy *Kugeln* was perfected. Glass ornaments were molded by blowing a bubble into a cookie mold. Soon glassblowers were producing pine cones, apples, pears, and crystal icicles for tree ornaments. In a short time they were being exported to America.

American store buyers, including F. W. Woolworth, began making side trips to Lauscha while scouting for toys and dolls in nearby Nuremberg and Sonneberg. Ornament-making totally dominated the life of Lauscha and the neighboring village of Steinheid.

By 1890 the Lauscha glassblowers had perfected the use of molds. The top and bottom halves of a mold were glued to a set of iron tongs. By the 1930s this had evolved into a handmade iron device with a steel spring which was clamped upright on the workbench. It held the mold at the right height and allowed the glassblower to open and close it with a pedal.

Reheating the closed end of a thin tube of glass which he had just sealed over his gas burner, the craftsman blew a bubble the same shape and only a little smaller than the ornament he was about to make. Quickly, he placed the still orange-hot molten bubble in the bottom half of the mold and closed the top, leaving only the blowing end of the tube protruding through a small hole. Working fast, before the glass could cool and always blowing downward into the mold, he expanded the thin glass bubble inside to fill the mold. After a few seconds, he opened the mold and a bird or acorn or some other recognizable shape emerged. The growing need for molds brought a new type of craftsmen to Lauscha—skilled artists or doll makers who could mold anything the American importers asked for.

Over the years, glassblowers of Lauscha reproduced every conceivable fruit and vegetable—even including several different pickles. Dogs, cats, monkeys, and bears abounded. Clowns and storybook characters were popular, as were the Christ child, angels, and the Christian symbol, the fish. A whole village of different little glass houses and churches could be hung on the tree, also objects like purses, pipes, drums, violins.

One of the most enduring patterns was the bird with a spun glass tail. Originally it hung from a delicate glass hook protruding from its back or head. By 1900 glassblowers had borrowed the clip from the clip-on candle holder of the period, and the birds acquired either one or two metal spring legs, which were soldered to the clip base before being glued into indentations in the bird's belly.

Many people remember or still have the fragile glass bird from grandmother's tree, but few have ever seen the many different kinds of birds that were originally made. In addition to a number of small birds native to Germany, unidentifiable to most Americans, there were cockatoos, parrots, owls, and the now extinct passenger pigeon. Regardless of species, most birds, including a peacock, had a two-inch tail made of hair-fine strands of spun glass. Those which didn't had a crinkly wire tail.

Santa Claus figures were always fashioned without legs, rounding off at the bottom of Santa Claus' coat. Santas from Lauscha almost invariably carried little Christmas trees. In the 1930s Czechoslovakian glassblowers imitated the German figures, but they never showed Santa Claus carrying a Christmas tree.

Enthusiasm for balloon ascensions gripped both Germany and the United States in the 1890s and was reflected in balloon-shaped ornaments, complete with wire-tinseled mesh ropes and embossed lithographic cutouts of angels and Santa Claus riding in the gondola. Motoring was similarly reflected on Christmas trees of the 1920s, when Lauscha glassblowers produced a tiny period car. And when the teddy bear craze gripped America, many teddies began appearing among the angels and Santa Clauses.

Some shapes were produced without molds. To make these, the glassblower pushed and pulled free-blown bubbles into different shapes while they were hot, using wooden tools and an asbestos covered leather glove. They blew tiny teapots and annealed delicate spouts and handles to them. In the same manner they made trumpets, as well as lyres, anchors, and butterfly bodies with spun glass wings. The toadstool, considered a sign of good luck in Germany, was a common object made without a mold. Trumpets that could be blown and bells that rang required the utmost craftsmanship, and one master craftsman blew, twisted, and coaxed a thin rod of glass into a delicate eight-inch stork which stood majestically on a Christmas tree.

In Lauscha, Friday was the day for marketing ornaments. Wives would strap towering baskets of them on their backs, often with additional bundles tied alongside, and off they would go, looking like blackbirds waddling with half-spread wings to catch the train for nearby Sonneberg where the warehouses were.

Traditionally, Monday was the day for the men to go to town to buy their supplies. But by the 1930s the system had begun to change. It was more efficient to have the collectors they worked for supply the glass rods and the five-gallon cans of lacquer, delivering these by truck. In some cases the collector's truck also began to call for the big baskets of ornaments. Woolworth, Kresge, Kress, and America's largest independent importer, Max Eckardt, all had warehouses near

Sonneberg; glassblowers now worked for one company.

The finished boxes of ornaments moved from Sonneberg by rail to the ports in the north of Germany. Steamship lines gave very good rates to America's ornament importers, for the lightweight Christmas tree balls made perfect "top cargo," filling the hold after it had almost reached its limit with heavy cargo.

The hard but somehow satisfying way of life of the glassblowers of Lauscha was totally disrupted in 1939. After the war the town found itself about 10 miles inside of East Germany. In 1949, in an effort to help the West German economy, the United States sent Max Eckardt and one of his sons to try to establish an ornament industry there. A number of Lauscha refugees lived in the Coburg area, only about 20 miles from their old homes, and there was still a market for the fragile, hand-blown and decorated ornaments.

So between 1950 and the early 1960s about 20 percent of America's ornaments were again imported from Germany. A school for glassblowers was started in Neustadt, West Germany, only a mile from the border, and the old Lauscha men trained up to 15 young glassblowers a year. But the work was hot and hard, and as the West German economy boomed, there was too much "quick money" to be made elsewhere, with medical insurance and pensions thrown in. If an ornament-maker's son wanted to follow his father's trade, his sweetheart would remind him, "Hans already owns a Volkswagen, and you have only a motor scooter." Few young girls in the new Germany dreamed of working as hard as the cottage workers' wives had.

About 600 glassblowers and their families moved to West Germany by sneaking through the woods on dark nights. Among those who stayed in Lauscha, a 10-year-long black market in Christmas tree ornaments developed. On foggy nights Lauscha men stealthily carried bundles of their fragile glass ornaments, rolled in tablecloths, to silent border meetings where they were slipped under the barbed wire. In return they got razor blades, coffee, cigarettes, and other commodities hard to obtain in the Eastern Zone.

By the 1960s, times had improved on both sides of the border, but, East or West, the ornament-makers continued to have little except the satisfaction of their work. Today in West Germany, fewer people make ornaments by hand with every passing year. And in Lauscha only a few old men, too old to work regularly, still blow ornaments in their homes. Others blow them on a production line at the town's government factory. They may even use a number of their old molds. But few of these fragile, fanciful ornaments now find their way to America, where the Christmas tree is ever more likely to be decked with plastic.

Friendship's Silent Sentinel

(The Martha Tree)

Tonight I trim the tree,
each ornament a gift from you. Lost
in deep memories I dream of yesterday,
today, tomorrow:
I, in the here and now;
you, in the Church Triumphant.
And yet a heavenly alchemy unites us evermore.

The tree still reaches high, from floor
to where it brushes highest ceiling. And there
your first gift nestles in pine-scented
greens: it is a chrismon fish, pure white,
blazoned with golden letters, IXTHUS, meaning
Jesus Christ. In Bethlehem his birth
became the blessed miracle that crowned our friendship.

Three golden birds (you brought them mid-December
as I trimmed the tree) hang to one side,
symbolic of the golden days I spent with you.
Tonight three memories shine in my heart
because of them: long walks on winter's snow-hushed
nights; the day you brought a multitude of
small white chrismon crosses for
the tree (I hang them now);
trimming our church together with the
greens of life in midst of winter, symbol
of faith and hope reborn. These are the birds
of gold that shine tonight like galaxies
outlined in fire of gold.

The tree, all fully trimmed, stands straight and tall,
and every ornament our friendship's "yes"
to yesterday and what is yet to be.
All sorrows blend spontaneously with sweet
content. And as the new dawn slowly breaks
"the morning stars sing out together.
And all the sons of God (I, in the here and now,
you, in the Church Triumphant)
shout for joy!"

—MELVA ROREM

26

Miracles, Folk Fancies, and the Christ Child

LOIS RAND

Illustrations by
William Medcalf

ENGLAND

THE Christmas story is the story of a miracle. But it is a miracle clothed in simple, human garb. How can we recognize a miracle disguised in ordinary, day-by-day events? How can we understand it? How can we appropriate it?

From the moment the shepherds were alerted on the starry hillside, or the Bethlehem residents began to spread strange talk in the streets, or Joseph and Mary pondered the adoration of the Wise Men, human beings have struggled to take this miracle into their minds and hearts. They have sought a framework for an event too big for a frame. They have tried to tell the story in language which is bound by words that are (simply because they are words) narrow, concise, and limited. For however it is said, the mind cannot express the mysteries which the heart can somehow understand.

Lonely, struggling persons have lived for centuries in the situation the miracle came to answer. They have needed security, healing, and restoration. They have craved for food and light that would satisfy not only for the moment, but forever. When people have not known the Christmas message, they have used natural events and their own native longings to build makeshift reassurances. From these gropings have grown centuries of folklore.

As the miracle of Christ's coming has been heard and understood and accepted, old fears and longings have been replaced with hope and surety. Old tales and customs have been adapted so they will reflect the good news of Christmas and keep its meaning alive. Countless traditions have surrounded the story often shared by several countries but adjusted to local circumstances. Each tells old truths.

SCOTLAND

BAVARIA

ENGLAND

The Holly and the Ivy

Old English tales reflect an unusual awareness of plants as reminders of God's great work. The holly and the ivy have long been used in Britain, both singly and together, to speak of healing and protection.

Because the holly bore fruit all winter, it came to symbolize immortality. It was hung at windows and doors as a token of protection against the fearful witches of pagan lore. One legend says that on the first Christmas Eve, a little lamb, following the shepherd to the manger, was caught in holly thorns and its drops of blood froze on the branches. Another says that Christ's crown of thorns was made of holly, and the berries were drops of his blood.

The ivy leaves were said to resemble God's footprint as he walked upon the earth to rescue us. The holly and the ivy, when used together, spoke of God's entry into history at a specific place, the suffering and bloodshed of Christ, and the eternal protection from evil which these events brought to the world.

The Glastonbury Thorn

One of England's strangest Christmas legends began with Christ's passion. It was said that once when Christ rested in the woods while enemies pursued him, birds covered him with hawthorn branches to conceal him. In remembrance of this, Joseph of Arimathea, who gave his tomb for Christ's burial, chose a hawthorn staff to take on a missionary journey which led eventually to Glastonbury, England. There he thrust the staff into the ground where it took root, put forth leaves, and bore flowers on Christmas Eve.

A further chapter was added to this story during an 18th century calendar controversy, when a change was proposed to alter the date of Christmas by 12 days. A caretaker of the Holy Thorns abbey in Glastonbury wrote a protest to the king and aroused much interest. When the newly scheduled Christmas Day arrived, 2000 persons came to see if the Glastonbury thorn was blooming. Finding it without so much as a bud, they agreed this couldn't be the right day for Christmas, and refused to carry on the usual festivities. Twelve days later, on the former Christmas date, the thorn bloomed, and the old calendar was restored.

This thorn was often carried in Christmas processions, and pilgrimages were made to the Holy Thorns abbey, for it was claimed that touching the thorns would remove evil and disease.

SCOTLAND

Midnight Magic

Scots believed that Christ was born at midnight on Christmas Eve, and that it was also at midnight that he turned water to wine at the Cana wedding. Reflecting human desire to see God's power in daily tasks, they believed that if anyone carried a bucket of water from the river at midnight, it would become wine.

Christmas Birthdays

Acknowledging that God's power is also available in our struggle against the persistent evils of life, Scottish lore claimed that persons born on Christ's birthday would be able to see spirits invisible to others, and would have power over them.

BAVARIA

Blessing the Cattle

Devout Bavarian farmers said that every Christmas Eve the cattle knelt at midnight in adoration of the Christ child. For a short while on this night, they were given the gift of speech to express their adoration. Because of this blessing, cattle received special attention from their owners each Christmas Eve.

The Little Stranger

One of the best-known Bavarian Christmas stories tells of a poor woodcutter and his family who were eating their meager Christmas Eve supper when they heard a knock at the door. Opening it, the woodcutter found a ragged, hungry child, half-frozen in the snow.

Filled with concern, the woodcutter brought the waif inside to feed and warm him. One of the sons slept on the stone hearth so the little stranger could have a soft bed. When the stranger fell asleep, the family said a prayer of gratitude for each other and their warm home.

At dawn, they were awakened by beautiful music. Looking outside, they saw the child, dressed not in rags but in shining garments, surrounded by a chorus of angels singing. He said, "I am the Christ child who brings blessings to loving hearts." Taking a branch from their little fir tree, he thrust it in the snow, and it burst forth with a covering of lights, silvery apples, and golden threads. "From this day on," he said, "when your tree bears fruit, it will be my birthday." The Christmas tree stood forever after as an eloquent reminder that "inasmuch as ye have done it unto one of the least of these, my brethren, ye have done it unto me."

DENMARK

SWEDEN

DENMARK

Blessing the Orchards

The Danes attached a miraculous importance to Christmas Eve. At midnight, farmers would go through their orchards, striking each tree, asking it to rejoice and be fruitful during the coming year. Thus they acknowledged the importance of this day and its relationship to all that we own.

Welcoming Guests

In Denmark, it became the tradition to make special Christmas cookies—many varieties of them—to be ready for guests. It was unthinkable that anyone who came to the home during the Christmas season would leave without enjoying cookies and a small glass of wine. If guests left unrefreshed, they would take Christmas away with them—a reminder that giving is the spirit of this holy season.

SWEDEN

Juletomte

The *Juletomte,* Sweden's equivalent of the Danish and Norse *Julenissen,* would come each Christmas Eve to attend the family feast, bringing gifts for everyone. He was a special, personal elf who watched over the household all year—its people and animals, its buildings and crops. As he sat watching in his special corner, he enjoyed the treat provided for him and gave his approval to the joyous celebration.

The Christmas Rose

One of the loveliest Swedish legends was set in the forest of Göinge. Long ago, on a Christmas Eve, all the birds, flowers, fruit, and trees of the forest awakened. For a few hours the plants grew, the birds sang, and the forest became a magical garden. Into this scene drifted the sound of mysteriously chiming bells and an angel chorus singing, "Glory to God in the highest."

Two churchmen walking by, observed the unusual sight, and decided it was the work of the devil. Because they doubted, all the beauty of the garden vanished, except for one lone flower which may still be seen in the forest at Christmastime. It is the Christmas rose which blooms each year, reminding all who see it of the beauty, strength, and purity of the Christ child.

NORWAY

The Yule Log

The "land of the midnight sun" in June is also the "land of the midday dark" in December. During this period when there was almost no daylight and the Vikings couldn't go to sea, they celebrated the pagan festival, Yule. They would gather in their great halls to feast and toast the gods. Bringing the largest log they could find, they blessed it, prayed over it, lit it, and tended it so it would burn for days. Around it, they celebrated as they awaited the return of the sun, always keeping a piece of the log to kindle next winter's fire.

For people who knew so well what darkness was, the Christmas message of Christ, the light of the world, had special appeal, and they kept the Yule log symbolism in their Christmas celebrations.

Candlelight

The value of light made candles important in Norwegian Christmas life, too. They were used abundantly on tables, on the Christmas tree, and in the windows. Tall Christmas candles were made to burn a long time.

Early Norwegians believed that candlelight radiated special blessings. Personal belongings and household articles were placed where the light could touch them, blessing them, and casting a halo of benediction on the members of the household too. Farmers carried lighted Christmas candles into barns and stables, singeing the sign of the cross into the hair of the cattle for good fortune in the year ahead. Fresh straw was spread out to be shined on by candlelight, then gathered and strewn on the fields as an offering for a good harvest in the coming year.

While these tales and customs of years ago seem fanciful, crude, superstitious, or even pagan, they are all significant. They tell great truths about the Savior and his birthday in common ways that are easily grasped. We might call them parables.

They contain the miraculous elements present in the first Christmas and in Christmas today. They tell us

... that God entered the world in human form, bringing his divine power into the lowliest corners of everyday life;

... that he restores wholeness, defeats evil, brings light and blessing to all who receive him;

... that joy, thankfulness, and love for others spring up in those whose hearts respond with awe and wonder to the miracle at Bethlehem.

NORWAY

Christmas Belle, Ardy

Old Timer

Oscar H.

Smooth Sledding

NOW, PUMP!

A Picture Story by LEE MERO

CHRISTMASTIME IN THE VILLAGE

Relating a few incidents from an era when the "three R's" stood for Readin', Ritin' and 'Rithmetic instead of today's Rush, Restlessness and Retirement!

~ the Editor and the Artist!

THE DAY BEFORE CHRISTMAS VACATION

Iva   Polly

A snowstorm the night before meant the snowplow men would be out early clearing the walks that led to school

Children from the surrounding countryside "hooked" rides

Those wooden sidewalks brought children running when crews replaced broken boards in the summer

found a pretty button

A PENNY! Cora Urness

OR rode horse-back

OR just plain walked the mile or so to school~

SLOWPOKE

(and back, again)

Barbara   David

"Uppity type" lunch bucket

THAT, Junior, is a slate, a slate pencil and a damp sponge.

little d'lard pails toted a lot of lunches too

Lunch Time brought on an active market in the trading of holiday cookery

Jeff   TRADE?   ?

Debbie

CHRISTMAS VACATION DAYS

With school out, youngsters came in handy around a home

comin', mamma

Little Boys ran errands

Lois and Sids new 3,000.00 house was one of the village "sights"

And wasn't it surprising how willing they were to Run ERRANDS and FETCH COAL and SIFT ASHES and SHOVEL SNOW

yes, mamma!

yes, papa!

("throw out the clinkers, son")

Little Mildred Lund had that "deft" touch with a turkey feather duster

yes, papa

THIS was WAY beyond one's imagination!

A well-stocked cellar meant plenty of "all the fixin's" for those holiday Jewell, Ia. meals

"Social Security", in those days, meant half a hog, a quarter of beef or a saddle of venison hanging in a well filled woodshed out behind the house

According to Mr. Kasberg "Now, this way, you've got what you want when you want it"

For spreading on home baked bread there was STRAW-, RASP-, HUCKLE-, or GOOSE-berry jelly, to say nothing of chokecherry and apple.

(Liked plain butter and brown sugar, myself)

AROUND THE VILLAGE

With special Christmas services in Sunday School and church coming up, Mr. Walter Schmidt thought it was time to take the boys to Mr. Schwarz's Tonsorial Parlor for "professional type" haircuts.

HAIRCUTS 35¢
SHAVE 15¢
BATHS 25¢
SAT. NIGHT 50¢

THIS + THESE = HAIRCUT
USE NO HORSES
THIS TIME UP

— Misty

The boys of the Clint Schroeder family got a laugh from folks on Main Street with their home-made sleigh.

A "Swell" from the City in a Box Coat intrigued the Old Timers
— Irv Melbostad

BELMOND

Mr. Lindaas Station Agent

The rest of the year it was on a do-it-at-home-basis.

The depot platform was an exciting place during the holidays as "City Folks" came and went.

Young Borgendale wondered if he'd EVER get that Mitchell motor bicycle he saw in the hardware store window

the Adv. said, "Simple as a Buggy" And "Fifty miles for 10¢"

NORRIS GLASOE GENERAL MERCHANDISE
HELGESON
BOOTS and SHOES
B & C 4 C
J. ELLINGBOE DRY GOODS NOTIONS

Note: He had to settle for a pair of Winslow's skates

(they clamped on)

As the Transcript reported, (Quote) Main Street was thronged Saturday, as eager Christmas shoppers made last minute holiday purchases. (Unquote)

COMPANY FOR CHRISTMAS

Edgar Guest once wrote, "It takes a heap o' livin' in a house to make it home". Well, the Rogness house had plenty of that!

Holiday Surprise:— a bobsled load of rambling relations!

WELL, HERE WE ARE!

A holiday salute to the "Hired Girl" of this era! Without inducement of private TV, radio, "hi-fi" or bus fare, she cooked, baked, scrubbed, swept, cleaned, washed, ironed, trimmed lamp-wicks, cleaned lamp chimneys--and baby sat!

A WICK TRIMMER

So shone her good deeds

Arnie

WHOOF!

NOW, SMILE!

Seemed like there was always a couple of "nags" tied up to their fancy hitching post.

Deck   Star

Mrs. Arnie Peterson's dining room was practically a Bower of Bells during the holidays. And there was always a cut glass bowl of delicious Raspberry Shrub on hand.

Many an otherwise gay gathering was ruined by a "Camera Fiend" and his flashlight apparatus!

The "NOW-WHAT-DO-WE-DO-WITH-EM" articles (as of Dec. 26th)

NON-PRACTICAL APRONS

HAND PAINTED STOVE SHOVEL

Minne-haha Falls

CHARCOAL PORTRAIT of Uncle Irving

BURNT LEATHER match safe and SCRATCHER

And Burned UP candles

(a requested reprint)

Home for Christmas
Garnet Hazard

Myriads of lights shine in Solvang on Christmas Eve.

Christmas in Little Denmark

JEAN LOUISE SMITH

IF YOU want to celebrate an authentic Danish Christmas without leaving the country, make plans to spend the holidays in Solvang, California. *Solvang* means "sunny field," and the Danish-Americans who settled there brought the sunshine and merriment, the charm and fantasy of their native country to the heart of the Santa Ynez Valley of Southern California. All year long, but especially at Christmas and during "Danish Days" (the third weekend in September) they lace their Danish festivities with the joyous interpretation of life found in "old Denmark."

Experience in Solvang the sudden impact of old-world Danish architecture. Observe the gleaming peaked copper roofs. Notice other residences where the roofs, shingled in a manner that resembles thatching, make the Danish-Americans who live there feel quite at home. Enjoy colorful shop windows that display handsome Danish products. Discover as you wander through the town that Solvang is indeed synonymous with Denmark in many ways.

The genuineness of this Danish environment evolves from the fact that a large number of the 2500 residents are descendants of those who settled there in the early 1900s. And the spirit and customs of the early settlers prevail. Over cobblestone pavements a horse-drawn car, the *høne* (the hen) clatters by, driven by a coachman wearing tight trousers, a long-tailed coat, and a high silk hat, straight from the pages of Denmark's great storyteller, Hans Christian Andersen. A park named in Andersen's honor contains a sculpture of him, and there are huge cutouts in stores and on street corners of characters from his stories. Everywhere there are large poster-like cutouts of the *Julemanden*, Denmark's Father Christmas, too, and his *Nisser*, small elves who assist him with his work as they perform unnumbered acts of love and add a mischievous deed here and there.

There are over 30,000 Danes in California, and Solvang contains the largest concentration of them. The town, lying about 35 miles northeast of Santa Barbara,

45

cannot be reached by plane, train, or bus—only by automobile. Visitors park their cars and take to the streets to explore the town by foot—the only way to absorb the uniquely Danish sights and sounds. Everywhere the air is fragrant with the odor of baking, and the sight of Danish goodies in bakery windows tempts the visitor to buy some to take home, or to sit down and have a cup of coffee with "a Danish" or two. There is an abundance of indoor and outdoor restaurants that feature smørgasbords, open-faced sandwiches, and other special foods. Inns and motels ably handle the influx of visitors.

Impressions come fast as you wander through the village area which is concentrated in a few square blocks of shops and restaurants and inns. Every inch is fresh and clean. Early in the morning shopkeepers are out with brooms and buckets—scouring, scrubbing. Life-sized, make-believe storks perch on roofs here and there, for in Denmark storks are regarded as harbingers of happiness. Bright colors are everywhere, with red and white, the national colors of Denmark, predominating. In the homes, warm, subdued reds contrast with clear blues. Wood panelings and moldings and provincially designed Danish furniture are in abundance.

In 1910, two Danish pastors, Benedict Nordentoft and J. M. Gregersen, and a Danish professor, P. P. Hornsyld, began the search for a site for a Danish folk school on the West Coast. As they looked over 9000 acres that seemed ideally suited for their purpose, which had been advertised for sale in Santa Barbara County, they were convinced that this was the right place for their settlement. The property was purchased, and newspaper ads were run in Danish settlements throughout the Middle West. Families quickly began purchasing plots and moved to Solvang.

Most families lived at first in a large rambling hotel, storing their furniture in a nearby hastily-built warehouse. At once, these strong, young Danes, superbly able to cope with rugged life and hard work, built homes. Soon construction began on the folk school, which they called Atterdag, and part of this building was used for a church. In 1914, they built a larger school, Atterdag College, which stood for 56 years on a hill overlooking the town. Courses were offered in Danish gymnastics, folk dancing, and various subjects important to Danish life and philosophy. The school ceased operation in 1937, but its spirit lives on in the life of the village today.

Three weeks before December 25th, shop windows are unveiled. At a given hour, window shades are taken down and lights are turned on throughout the village and on the Christmas tree in the park. The atmosphere is festive and most of the villagers wear native costumes. The band plays and there is folk dancing in the streets.

Fair-haired girls in native dress welcome everyone.

Danish-styled Bethania Lutheran Church.

Country-style windmills inspire joyous dancers.

King Merrill Photos

In the shops the best of Danish goods have been stocked on shelves and displayed in windows: fine glassware, the familar Danish Christmas plates, china, ceramics, linens, embroidered and handwoven fabrics, toys, copper and enamel kettles—every item of high quality.

Elaborate preparations have been going on in the homes too. Every young child has a special Christmas calendar, usually made of fabric, with the child's name gaily embroidered at the top. Under each date father and mother have hung a surprise gift, and opening these gifts each day is almost as exciting as opening gifts under the tree on Christmas Eve.

Every day kitchens are filled with the aroma of Christmas baking. There are special pastries and dishes that are always prepared ahead of time. Dozens of cookies, cakes, and other confections are made for the family and to delight friends who drop in. Some of these special recipes are included on these pages.

Ferdinand Sorensen has strongly influenced the development of the town. A gifted artist, he and his wife, Gudrun, live there in an authentically Danish provincial-style house on Old Mill Road. Appropriately, it is named *Møllenkken,* Mill on the Hill, after the first windmill built in Solvang.

When Sorensen moved to Solvang in 1933, he soon envisioned it as a Danish town. He made frequent trips to Denmark where he studied characteristics of their architecture: the use of cross beams, thatched and copper roofs, the use of wood panelings and moldings, and the design of Danish provincial furniture. Soon he was devoting all his time to designing and building Danish-style shops and homes. He is largely responsible for the entire layout of the center of the town.

It is a Danish fairyland, exuding joy and charm.   King Merrill Photo

On each trip to Denmark he tried to secure a work of art portraying the storyteller, Hans Christian Andersen. Finally, he heard through the Danish ambassador in New York, that there is a plaster cast of a sculpture in Los Angeles, California. This is a bust taken from a full-figure made in bronze by Henry Luckow Nielsen in Denmark. Sorensen has now persuaded Nielsen to cast the plaster in bronze in Denmark and ship it to Solvang where it will be prominently displayed.

An outstanding example of Danish architecture and another landmark of Solvang, Bethania Lutheran Church, was designed by one of the village's first resident architects, Hans C. D. Skytt. He followed the style of Grundtvig's Church in Copenhagen, reproducing the same slanting, step-like crenulations for the roof and tower. The Copenhagen church remains unique, however, in that its facade resembles a huge pipe organ of brick and glass—a fitting memorial to Nikolai Grundtvig, Denmark's greatest hymnwriter.

The simple interior of Bethania Church is light in color. Above the altar is a fine, large replica of Thorvaldsen's sculpture, *Christ.* Interestingly, the figure came from Alden, Minnesota. When Carlston Lutheran Church there was struck by lightning and burned, the Danish parishioners offered the rescued statue to the church at Solvang.

Suspended from the ceiling of the church, halfway down the nave, is a large model of a sailing ship. A ship is a traditional symbol in Denmark, and in Christian symbolism it represents the soul of the Christian making its way on the waters of the sea of life, with God's guidance, to safe harbor.

On Christmas Eve the church is decorated with festive greens and candles, and entire families—children, parents, grandparents, aunts, uncles—and other members and visitors, gather for the traditional Danish service. The old country's hymns ring out in the old country's language, and scripture verses, meditations, and prayers are spoken in Danish. The present pastor is the Reverend Carlo Petersen.

HANS CHRISTIAN ANDERSEN

47

After the service, greetings of *"Glædelig Jul!"* (Merry Christmas) resound as members leave the church and go to their homes to enjoy festive dinners. Myriads of Christmas lights shine from the dormers and along the facades of the Danish-type buildings. The Christmas goose has been stuffed with prunes and apples and will soon be ready to serve with browned potatoes and fluffy rice. Red cabbage *(Rødkål)* is always a delight, not only at Christmas but throughout the year. Almond pudding *(Ris Almande)* is served for dessert. Chopped almonds are added and also a whole almond. The person who finds the whole almond in his pudding is given a prize or is honored by receiving the first gift. A large plate of Christmas cookies, apple cake, fruits, and nuts are passed to complete the meal.

Later, family and friends join hands and form a circle around the tree as it casts its age-old splendor over everything. Then a moment of silence falls, and every hour of preparation—the baking, the cleaning, the planning, the scheming—seem to point to this hour. And yet, did they not stand against the background of father reading the Christmas story, customary in so many homes, the moment would not be so shining. The most loved carols are sung. The tree, often standing in the center of the room, has been lovingly trimmed with festoons of small paper Danish flags, cone-shaped cornucopias filled with small candies, tiny wreaths, garlands of bells made from colored paper or foil, and family ornaments treasured through the years.

As last the moment comes for the tree to yield the mysterious, packaged treasures it has claimed until this moment. There are gifts for everyone, of course. Wrappings are excitedly torn off, and in what seems a sudden moment the room knows the delightful disorder that is normally expected every Christmas Eve.

Christmas Day in Solvang, as in Denmark, is a quiet day, with no special activities planned. It is a day of reflection on the days and weeks of expectation and preparation, and now the *experience* of Christ's coming again to earth. For he comes indeed!

Christmas everywhere. . . . Christmas in Bethania Lutheran Church. Christmas in the home. And most of all, Christmas in the heart.

RIS ALMANDE
(Rice and Almond Pudding)

3½ cups milk	1 whole almond
3½ tablespoons sugar	1/3 cup sherry wine
¾ cup long grain white rice	2 teaspoons vanilla
1 cup blanched almonds, chopped	½ pint chilled whipping cream

Bring milk to boil. Add sugar and rice, stir, and lower heat. Simmer uncovered for 30 minutes, until rice is tender. Pour into a bowl and add chopped almonds, the whole almond, sherry, and vanilla. Cool. Whip cream and fold into rice mixture. Chill well before serving. The pudding may be served with fruit sauce or frozen strawberries if you wish.

Earlier, in Denmark, a bowl of the pudding was put on the porch or in the barn for the *Nisser.* If the pudding was gone by morning, the household would have good luck during the coming year.

STEGT JULEGASS
(Christmas Goose)

10-12 pound goose, fresh or frozen
2 pounds apples, peeled and quartered
1 pound prunes, soaked, pitted, chopped
Salt, flour

After the goose has thawed, wash inside and outside with warm water. Remove pinfeathers. (Boil giblets and set aside for giblet gravy if desired.) Rub cavity with salt and stuff with apples and prunes.

Place on a rack in roaster and prick all over with sharp tines of fork. Roast in 450° oven for about 45 minutes. Remove and drain all fat from roaster. Sprinkle goose with salt and dredge with flour. Return to oven and lower temperature to 350°. Allow about 15 minutes more per pound roasting time. Sprinkle goose with flour lightly about every 30 minutes to help absorb goose grease. When browned nicely and leg joint moves easily, remove from oven. Let stand at least 30 minutes before serving. It may be served with red cabbage and small boiled whole potatoes which can be browned in goose fat and brown sugar in a heavy skillet, mixing ½ cup of goose fat with 2 tablespoons brown sugar.

RØDKAAL
(Red Cabbage)

3-pound head red cabbage	2 tablespoons sugar
¼ cup butter	½ cup water
4 tablespoons vinegar	2 tablespoons red current jelly

Remove and wash outer leaves of cabbage. Shred or quarter cabbage and drain well. Melt butter in heavy saucepan, add cabbage, and toss well with wooden spoon to coat cabbage evenly. Add vinegar and water. Cover tightly and simmer 20 to 30 minutes, until cabbage is just tender. Mix jelly, sugar, and salt and stir into cabbage. Cook 5 or 10 minutes more to blend flavors. Prepare a day ahead and reheat before serving.

Aromas of Danish delights fill the air.

Christmas Music Stamps

LEE KLEINHANS

The wonderful world of stamps entices a host of collectors. Interest may persist for a lifetime in this endless venture of seeking and finding. For just over the next hill lies added information and new inspiration. And around the next corner you may find a long-sought treasure. You have only to know for what you are looking, and there is the ever-present chance that you will find it.

One of the most fascinating forms of collecting is the search for a special classification, the "subject" or "topical" stamp collection. Of these, one of the most interesting is the Christmas music stamp collection that tells through music the story of the Christ child's birth. These stamps have become extremely popular and are issued even in non-Christian countries simply as a commercial venture.

Some collectors narrow their search for Christmas music stamps to miniature reproductions of great works of Christian art that have a musical theme. Many other stamps are related to the musical celebration of Christmas. We see stamps that picture choirs of angels, carolers who go from door to door, composers, familiar melodies, well-known lyrics, and musical instruments that include harps, drums, trumpets, shawms, bells, tambourines, vielles, bagpipes, lutes, and flutes.

HUNGARY 1943

LIECHTENSTEIN 1962

UNITED STATES 1965

MALTA 1969

UNITED STATES 1972

BRAZIL 1968

GREAT BRITAIN 1972

ITALY 1973

AUSTRIA 1948

AUSTRIA 1968

GREAT BRITAIN 1970

MALAWI 1969

COSTA RICA 1960

UNITED STATES 1971

BAHAMAS 1973

BAHAMAS 1972

Christmas stamps suggest all the elements of adoration and praise related to Christmas that we have known and hold dear: happy sounds, rejoicing, glad celebration, high festivity, gathering of families and friends with jollity and feasting. Times of remembering, too. . . . Yesterday, the old, old songs, childhood and growing-up days, Christmas Past.

Luke's account of the Savior's birth does not mention singing. He tells of the multitude of heavenly angels praising God and *saying*, "Glory to God in the highest, and on earth peace among men with whom he is pleased." Through the centuries, we have come to speak of this as the angels' *song*. Because we celebrate his birth with song, we somehow assume that there must have been music on that night in Bethlehem.

A Hungarian stamp of 1943 is the first to show the angels making their announcement to the shepherds with musical instruments. Their good tidings appear on Australia's 1961 stamp issued for the 350th anniversary of the publication of the King James translation of the Bible.

The angels who appeared to the shepherds keeping watch over their flock in the fields near Bethlehem may be thought of as history's first carolers. And if we construe this as "the angels' song," their message to the shepherds can be considered the first Christmas carol.

"I heard the bells on Christmas Day," the poem written by Henry Wadsworth Longfellow in 1863 when his son lay seriously wounded in the Civil War, speaks of another kind of Christmas music.

> I thought of how, as day had come,
> The belfries of all Christendom
> Had rolled along th' unbroken song
> Of peace on earth, good will to men.

The most famous Christmas belfry belongs to the Church of the Nativity in Bethlehem. Each Christmas its bell peals for thousands of pilgrims who come to Bethlehem to celebrate the anniversary of the Savior's birth.

Even Santa Claus gets into the Christmas music scene on the United States' stamp of 1972 where he holds a small trumpet. Native African drums appear in a less secular setting on the 1963 Christmas stamp of the Vatican. They picture a native African nativity scene based on a terra cotta plaque by Andreas Bukuru of Burundi.

"Silent night" is probably the world's best-known, best-loved carol. It has been the subject of two Austrian stamps. The first was issued in 1948 for the 130th anniversary of the composition of the hymn. It pictures Father Joseph Mohr, who wrote the words, and organist Franz Gruber, who composed the music.

The carol might never have been written if the organ had not broken down in the little wooden church in the Bavarian hamlet of Oberndorf on Christmas Eve, 1818. "We can never have Christmas without music," said Father Mohr. So while the wind shrieked in the chimney and rattled the doors and windows of the church, Father Mohr seated himself at his table in the small bare room at the back of the church. Slowly, slowly, the muse spoke to him.

> Silent night, holy night,
> All is calm, all is bright. . . .

Darkness had fallen when the last words were written, and he hurried to show them to composer Gruber. Gruber read them again and again, and soon he was humming a little melody. It fit the words and, while old Hans, the village cobbler, strummed the simple chords on his guitar, the young, fresh voices of the mountain singers learned the tune and the lyrics. There was music — a lovely new song that has never been forgotten—at their midnight Christmas Eve service that night.

For the sesquicentennial of the carol, Austria issued a stamp in 1968 showing the crèche in the Memorial Church at Oberndorf near Salzburg.

Charles Wesley and Felix Mendelssohn are responsible for the carol, "Hark! the herald angels sing." The title appears across the top of a 1969 stamp from Christmas Island, its first Christmas stamp, which pictures an angel playing a harp.

Wesley wrote the words of this hymn, the most famous of his 6000 hymns, in 1739. His words were first used with the Mendelssohn melody in 1855, after both men had died. Mendelssohn wrote the music as part of a choral work, for the tercentenary of the invention of the art of printing, a tribute to Johann Gutenberg. He never intended it to be used with sacred words; in fact, he said as much while musing that the tune might become popular if secular words were written for it.

"O come all ye faithful, joyful and triumphant" form the top and right margins of Australia's 1968 Christmas stamp, reproducing a

BOTSWANA 1972

CANADA 1967

JORDAN 1971

VENEZUELA 1972

UNITED STATES 1972

VATICAN CITY 1963

DOMINICAN REPUBLIC 1967-68

CHRISTMAS ISLAND 1969

AUSTRALIA 1960

AUSTRALIA 1963

AUSTRALIA 1968

AUSTRALIA 1961

Good King Wenceslas

Good King Wenceslas looked out,
On the feast of Stephen,
When the snow lay round about,
Deep and crisp and even.
Brightly shone the moon that night,
Though the frost was cruel,
When a poor man came in sight,
Gath'ring winter fuel.

"Hither, page, and stand by me,
If thou know'st it telling,
Yonder peasant, who is he?
Where and what his dwelling?"
"Sire, he lives a good league hence,
Underneath the mountain,
Right against the forest fence,
By Saint Agnes' fountain."

"Bring me flesh, and bring me wine,
Bring me pine logs hither:
Thou and I shall see him dine,
When we bear them thither."
Page and monarch, forth they went,
Forth they went together;
Through the rude wind's wild lament
And the bitter weather.

"Sire, the night is darker now,
And the wind grows stronger;
Fails my heart, I know not how;
I can go no longer."
"Mark my footsteps, my good page,
Tread thou in them boldly;
Thou shalt find the winter's rage
Freeze thy blood less coldly."

In his master's steps he trod,
Where the snow lay dinted;
Heat was in the very sod
Which the Saint had printed.
Therefore, Christian men, be sure,
Wealth or rank possessing,
Ye who now will bless the poor,
Shall yourselves find blessing.

view of Bethlehem as seen through the stone tracery of a cathedral window. The mystery of the carol has still to be solved. Copies of the words found in England in the handwriting of John Francis Wade, indicate he may have composed it. However, there is some feeling that it may have been written by an anonymous Frenchman, for it has long been popular in France where Wade worked as a music copyist. The music is sometimes called "The Portuguese Hymn," because it was played in the Portuguese embassy chapel in London in the 18th century. The organist there at the time thought the tune had probably been written by John Reading, organist at Winchester College, a century earlier.

Artist Jamie Wyeth chose "The twelve days of Christmas" as the theme for a United States Christmas stamp he designed in 1971. This old English folk carol deals with a popular aspect of Christmas gift-giving. It is conservatively estimated that the cost of the gifts given in this carol would be at least $20,000!

Other Christmas carols that would fit with stamps pictured on these pages are "O little town of Bethlehem," "While shepherds watched their flocks by night," and "Angels from the realms of glory."

More Christmas carols may appear on stamps in the wake of the popularity generated by Great Britain's impressive set depicting scenes from "Good King Wenceslas." King Wenceslas, the peasant, and his page are pictured on the 3½ pennys, each stamp representing a verse of the carol. The melody is a medieval tune for an old spring song. The words of the carol, written by the Reverend John Mason Neale, D.D.

Good King Wen - ces - las looked out, On the feast of Ste - phen,

When the snow lay round a - bout, Deep and crisp and ev - en.

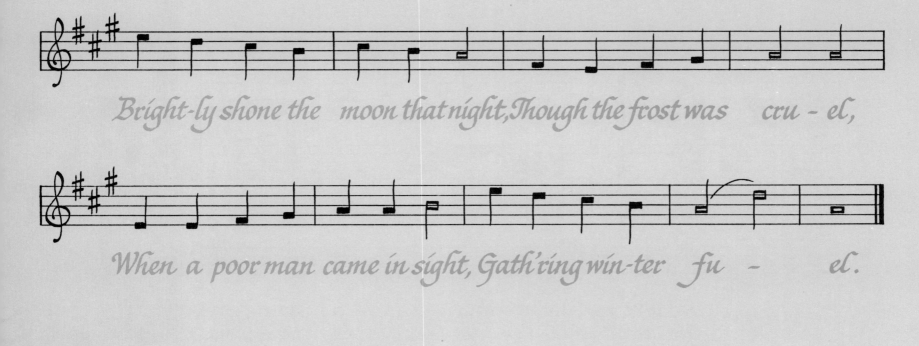

Bright-ly shone the moon that night, Though the frost was cru - el,

When a poor man came in sight, Gath'ring win-ter fu - el.

(1818-1866), and the illustrative stamps appear on the opposite page.

This carol from Bohemia tells a story about a wise and good nobleman named Duke Wenceslas. The good ruler was called King Wenceslas even though he was not a king. He was loved by all his people, for no matter what the hour of day or night, if he received word that one of his subjects was ill or in need, he hastened to help out at once. During the Christmastide, King Wenceslas made sure that there were celebrations in every church and every cottage in his dominion.

Wenceslas was martyred in his 20s for promoting faith and charity among his subjects. When this entailed a conciliatory policy toward his German neighbors, he was killed by his brother's supporters who opposed his foreign policy. St. Wenceslas is the patron saint of modern Czechoslovakia.

The opening lines of Psalm 100 catch the spirit that these music-related stamps tell as they go their way echoing God's praises round the world:

Make a joyful noise to the Lord,
    all the lands!
Serve the Lord with gladness!
Come into his presence with singing!

Christmastide is always a season of the heart. Heart speaks to heart in words as shouts of "Merry Christmas"—in whatever tongue—go from friend to friend; in deeds, as gifts are given; in song that fills the air from hill to plain to valley. Christmas music stamps bear the message too, from village to village, from city to city, from nation to nation: "Christ is born!"

WHEN CHRIST OUR LORD WAS BORN

John H. Payne

Traditional Sicilian
Arr. David N. Johnson

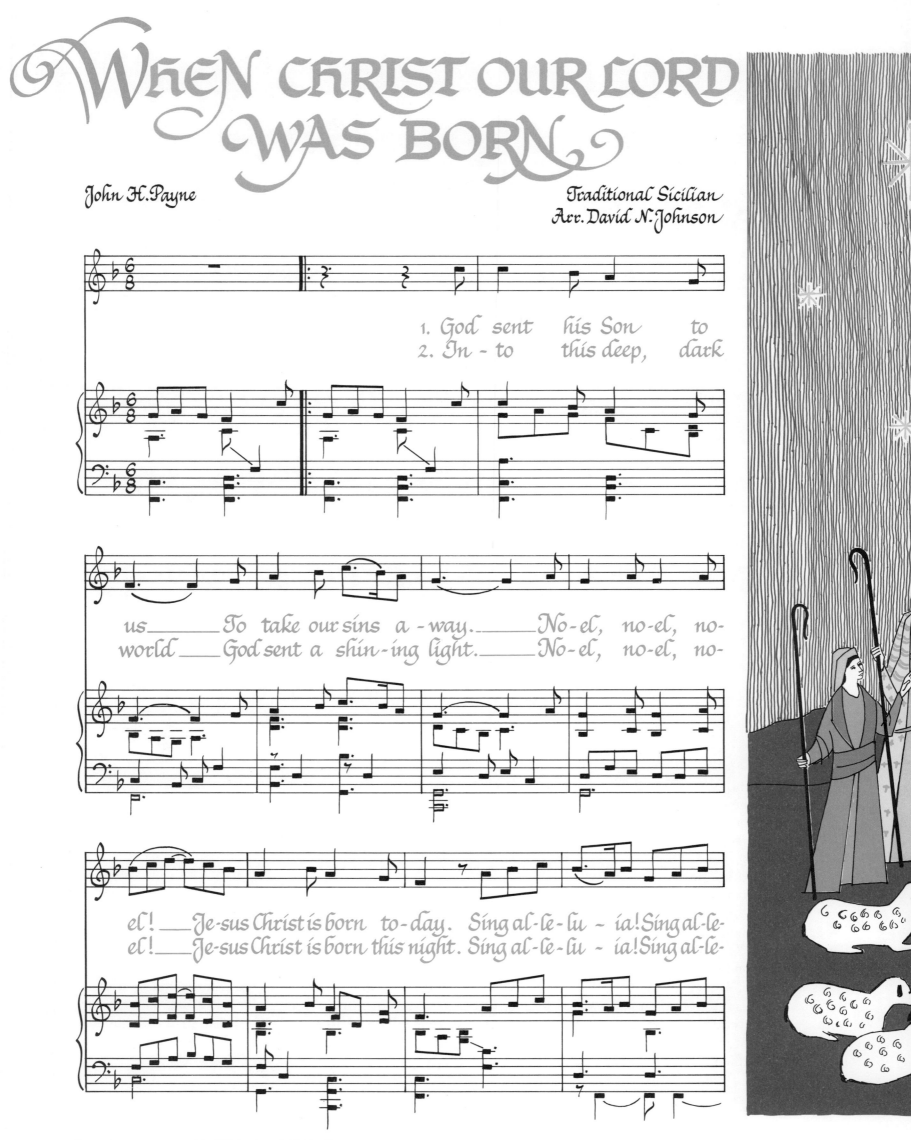

1. God sent his Son to us ____ To take our sins a - way. ____ No-el, no-el, no-el! ____ Je-sus Christ is born to-day. Sing al-le-lu ~ ia! Sing al-le-

2. In - to this deep, dark world ____ God sent a shin-ing light. ____ No-el, no-el, no-el! ____ Je-sus Christ is born this night. Sing al-le-lu ~ ia! Sing al-le-

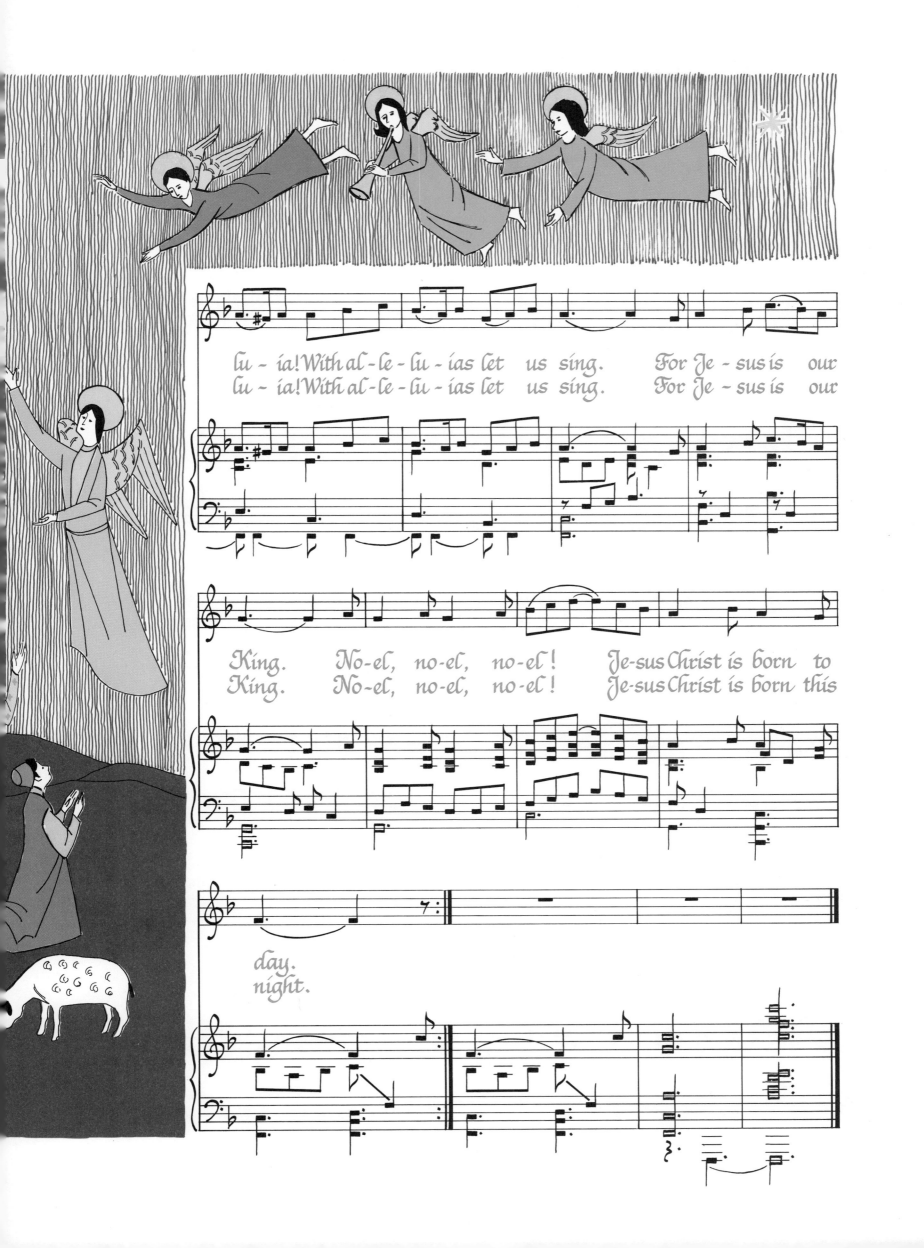

A CHILD IS BORN IN BETHLEHEM

Nikolai F. S. Grundtvig, 1783-1872
Tr. Frank Pooler

Traditional Danish
Arr. Carl Schalk

1. A child is born in Beth-le-hem, in Beth-le-hem. Great joy then in Je-ru-sa-lem. Al-le-lu-ia! Al-le-lu-ia!
Et barn er født i Bet-le-hem, i Bet-le-hem. Ti gle-der sig Je-ru-sa-lem. Al-le-lu-ia! Al-le-lu-ia!
2. The man-ger held the bless-ed boy, the bless-ed boy. God's an-gels sang a song of joy. Al-le-lu-ia! Al-le-lu-ia!
3. E-ter-nal thanks and praise we bring, all praise we bring; And to the ho-ly Three we sing Al-le-lu-ia! Al-le-lu-ia!

Now Found Is the Fairest of Roses

Hans Adolf Brorson, 1694-1764
Tr. J.C. Aaberg

Traditional Danish
Arr. Richard Hillert

1. Now found is the fair-est of ros-es; 'Mongst bri-ars it
2. All men should with glad-ness for-ev-er Give prais-es to
3. My Je-sus, thou ev-er re-main-est My glo-ry and

sweet-ly re-pos-es. My Je-sus so pre-cious and ho-ly
God for his fa-vor, But man-y have ne'er com-pre-hend-ed
crown, who sus-tain-est My heart in the full-ness of plea-sure;

A - bode a - mong sin - ners so low - ly.
The Rose to the world has de - scend - ed.
Thy sweet - ness a - lone will I trea - sure.

BRIGHT AND GLORIOUS IS THE SKY

Nikolai F.S. Grundtvig, 1783–1872
Tr. Service Book and Hymnal

Traditional Danish
Arr. Paul Manz

1. Bright and glo-rious is the sky, Ra - diant are the
2. On that ho - ly Christ-mas night, Through the dark-ness
3. As a star God's ho - ly Word Leads us to our

heav-ens high Where the gold-en stars were shin-ing,
beamed a light; All the stars a - bove were pal-ing,
King and Lord; Bright-ly from its sa - cred pa - ges

And their rays to earth in-clin-ing, Beck'n-ing us to
All their lus-ter slow-ly fail-ing As the Christ-mas
Shall this light through-out the a - ges Shine up - on our

THE HAPPY CHRISTMAS COMES ONCE MORE

Nikolai F. S. Grundtvig, 1783-1872
Tr. Charles Porterfield Krauth, 1823-1883

Carl C. N. Balle, 1806-1855
Arr. Judy Hunnicutt

1. The hap - py Christ - mas comes once more, The heav'n - ly
2. O wake, our hearts, in glad - ness sing, And keep our
3. Come, Je - sus, glo - rious heav'n - ly guest, Keep thine own

guest is at the door, The bless - ed words the shep - herds
Christ - mas with our King, Till liv - ing song, from lov - ing
Christ - mas in our breast. Then Da - vids harp-strings, hushed so

thrill, The joy - ous tid - ings, 'Peace, good-will.'
souls, Like sound of might - y wa - ter rolls.
long, Shall swell our ju - bi - lee of song.

Crèche by Feichtinger and Scheichl built between 1890 and 1913.

Salzburg's Crèche/Toy Exhibit

LA VERN J. RIPPLEY

ACCORDING to most people, the crèche scene is the kernel of Christmas as a religious holiday. Fundamentally, the crèche typifies the giving, loving, and sharing of ourselves with our neighbor at Christmastime. Toys, gifts — the costly business of exchanging presents — might be examples of the miserable materialism that has parasitically encroached on the true spirit of Christmas. After all, are not toys the tokens of secularism which, at an early age, filter into the minds of children to corrupt for them the real meaning of Christmas? Wrong! Wrong, at least according to contemporary researchers in Austria who have been re-examining the many facets of celebrating Christmas in the Salzburg region.

Toys, in the views of these young investigators, are not the symbols of materialism, and they must not be separated from Christmas understood in its religious sense. According to these Austrian scholars of folklore, tangible, concrete gifts — in particular, toys — belong to the bone marrow of Christmas as depicted so vividly in the crèche scene.

Scientific studies, initially inspired by faith, led the directors of Salzburg's regional museum, the Carolino Augusteum, to arrange an exhibit which manifests the interrelationship between the crèche and the toy. Both crèche scenes and toys were, for the first time in anyone's memory, displayed in such a way as to illustrate the intimate association between them. The exhibition of crèche scenes at the Salzburg Museum has been part of the museum's Christmas fare for many years. It has, in fact, been one of Europe's most distinguished "homes" for the evolution and exhibition of the crèche scene. The display, however, was the first time both crèche scenes and toys were combined in one overall exhibit. This action vividly manifests the results of scholarly investigations and conclusions which began with studies of the crèche: in other words, the crèche itself is viewed as nothing more than a toy.

The prime mover in making the crèche/toy exhibit a reality was Dr. Volker Kutschera, the museum's curator for theater history and director of informational services. Two of the primary writers on crèche creations in the Salzburg region are Barbara Kut-

Tin car from 1910-1920 with bisque headed doll from 1890-1900.

schera, Volker's wife, and Dr. Frederike Prodinger, a colleague and curator with Dr. Volker Kutschera on the staff of the Salzburg Museum. A number of their publications have appeared in the Innsbruck-based journal, *Der Krippenfreund,* as well as in several books published recently in Austria, where the subject of the crèche is explored in detail by a number of scholars. The primary sources for making the display we describe here a reality were, on the one hand, the Carolino Augusteum's own storerooms where the crèches which have been assembled over the years are kept, and, on the other hand, the toy collection of Hugo and Gabriele Folk, which the Salzburg Museum had acquired.

The Toys

Throughout all of their lives, Hugo and Gabriele Folk have been collecting toys. Totaling approximately 30,000 objects in all, the Folk Toy Collection, as it is now officially designated, is at present the largest compilation of historically significant toys in all of Austria. For over 40 years of their married lives, the Folks have been planting the seeds by searching and researching toys. This, with time, yielded a bountiful harvest.

The Folks had lived in Vienna. But with the dedication of their masterpiece collection to Salzburg's Carolino Augusteum, the Folks have moved their home from Vienna to Salzburg so they can live out their days in the proximity of their "children," the toys. Thus the museum has not only had the good fortune of acquiring title to the collection, but access to the Folks' expertise in toy making, toy psychology, and toy history. Scarcely anyone else has the "surgical" talent of Frau Folk when it comes to healing and mending the limbs of broken dolls or currying up scruffy toy animals. She is also not only a scholarly historian of toy clothing, native costumes, and many culturally significant details of long-forgotten toy styles, but she is also a masterful technician when it comes to tailoring new doll clothing in former styles,

remolding distorted tin figures, and reconstructing dilapidated dollhouses.

Likewise, Hugo Folk has demonstrated the skills of both an inventor and an engineer in putting the little "wrecks" back into mechanical operation. Stretching back over the last 200 years, such toys manifest a great deal more ingenuity than do modern electrically-powered metal toys found in our department stores. To be sure, the older models all had to be driven by one of two power sources—either the hand crank or the drive wheel—but the wooden carvings and artistic decorations of the old toys excel anything available in our time. Truly, they represent an art and a skill that has disappeared from the human repertoire of talents. As a representative of such a former talent treasury, Hugo Folk also has displayed impressive ability in collecting and maintaining a wealth of interesting paper theaters, complete with many scene changes.

Gabriele Folk started collecting toys in her early childhood. She was an only child and found companionship in the quiet of her parents' house by creating "friends" out of her own fantasy. Her playmates were her toys. Even at the tender age of five, Frau Folk recounts, she liked to gather all of her toys into

Wood carved crèche figure dressed as native of the region a century ago.

a compartmentalized box which she propped up in the form of a display in her room—as if this made her toys into "friends" who were perpetually and personally present with her.

Later, when Gabriele finished school, she studied with Professor Viktor Schufinsky, working as his assistant at the Vienna Art Institute. Here she perfected her artistic talent as well as the craftsman's skills needed for her lifetime vocation. For 20 years she continued working with Professor Schufinsky, absorbing from him some of his passion for toy collecting. As a result of this mutual cooperation, the major portion of Professor Schufinsky's own extensive toy collection came into the hands of his student, Gabriele. Together, the two collections were organized in glass display cases and categorized according to a system of family, genus, and species. To facilitate scientific research, a card catalog with cross-referencing now accompanies the collection, and an extensive set of files provides ready information on any item.

Hugo Folk's love of toys is intimately entwined with his fascination for theater. Toy collecting for him was the realization of a dream. He knew early in life that he needed an activity at home to relieve the tensions generated by an ulcer-threatening career with a large Vienna bank. Fortunately for him, Hugo explains, he had carried with him from childhood his security blanket—his penchant for toy collecting. At home, in the evenings and on weekends, he always used his toy release valve. Until his toy horizons expanded, Hugo was mainly interested in puppet theaters and paper figure actors.

Today the Folk Toy Collection has over 60 paper doll theaters; most of them are toy reproductions of real life stage sets. They depict in miniature actual

Interior of dollhouse.

productions from major theaters and dramas that have been played on the world's stages. Everything in Hugo's dollhouse theaters was once a genuine theater production. According to Hugo, there was once a tradition in theater history that major productions were announced and advertised to the public by doll-sized enactments of a given scene from an upcoming production. These doll scenes were previews of the real thing; the doll shows accurately mirrored the stage sets of a specific drama. Sometimes these dolls and theater scenes were duplicated many times to facilitate the job of advertising. When the play's run was well underway, the doll sets were often sold between acts at performances. Here, parents who went to the theater, eagerly bought them to take home.

Obviously, then, the Folk Collection is much more than just a toy collection. Rather, it presents through select examples, a visually-aided history of European culture. The Collection's 300-year time span of toys and theaters depicts in mirror and in miniature the

Rag dolls and animals.

Russian troika, Folk Collection.

same 300-year span of cultural history. Not limited to national boundaries, the Collection portrays many of the quilt-patch Hapsburg lands that made up the Central European Austrian empire. But it also houses objects from northern Europe and Russia, as well as from Sicily and Portugal. There are also a few toys from the Orient.

Variety is a trademark of the Collection. There are examples ranging from the finest tiny tin figures to large, robust rocking horses. Tiny steam locomotives grind up mountains on a cogwheel track, and dolls prepare meals, do the laundry, and bake bread in kitchens and houses equipped with the best period furnishings. Market day in toy town scenes is as colorfully reminiscent of the horn of plenty as is the real thing on Salzburg's streets, still only a block away from the museum. Salzburg's grocery stores display their foods far differently today, but many of the sausages, apples, baked goods, and candies in the stores on the streets look very much like those carved wooden miniatures on the shelves of the dollhouse stores in the museum glass cases. True, in virtually every detail to the actual street scenes, are the miniature Christkindlmarkt booths that line the streets of Salzburg (and many other cities in the German-speaking areas of Europe) during the weeks before Christmas. Some specialize in foods, others in baked goods, some in Christmas tree decorations, others in meats or fruits. A few of the toys have strongly religious overtones, such as Noah's Ark. What is atypical about the ark is that it is carved of wood in the precise style of an Alpine barn—reflecting much more the local folkloric traditions than fidelity to the biblical description of Noah's Ark.

Although a mere pipe dream at the moment, specialists at the Salzburg Museum hope someday to reproduce some of the more fascinating toys in the Folk Collection so that they may not only be seen,

64

but actually played with by children. The museum would like to establish a play room in which parents could deposit their children while they visit exhibits not of interest to youngsters. The children would get a set of tokens which they could use to check out replicas of the museum's toys for their own learning and handling pleasure.

A strong folkloric motif pervades all of the crèche scenes. Instead of Middle East buildings and clothing styles, the scenes in the Salzburg crèches are distinctly Alpine and South German in character. Likewise, the Christ child is usually born in a typical *Bauernhof* that looks like the farmsteads that speckle the Alpine countryside in the region. Occasionally, a crèche scene includes not only the traditional Bethlehem figures, but personages from an entire village. In such cases, the villagers are depicted feasting at an outdoor table decked with local foods.

Studies have shown that whole-village crèche scenes were actually satires designed to mock the human weaknesses of villagers and town officials. On at least one occasion in Salzburg's history, such a crèche scene satirized the church hierarchy in the Salzburg area. This attack was met in 1782 by a decree in the form of a pastoral letter from Archbishop Hieronymus forbidding further use of the crèche in any form. When strong protests spontaneously arose

The carousel crèche mounted on pole.

among the common people, the bishop backed away from his total ban. He allowed small, simple crèche scenes to be used in homes, provided there were no more "silly, clumsy, childish figures in the scenes." In general, whole-village scenes are furnished in the Alpine tradition. Occasionally, however, as one's eye glides beyond the festivities closer to the nativity scene, a few palm trees and other Middle East trappings grace the landscape.

One crib worthy of special note in the museum is made of Salzburg china, the *Fayence Crèche*, crafted by Trude Hillinger in 1941. An even more singular example of the Salzburg art of crèche making is the *Drehkrippe zum Sternsingenlaufen*, the carousel crèche made by members of the guild of shippers from Oberndorf and Laufen. Built about 1800, a set of gears made of carved wood rotate the crèche scene which is mounted on the top of a pole. As the scene revolves, its intricately carved wooden figures are displayed for all to see. The revolving crèche figures were carried during ceremonies on January 6th, when carolers made the rounds carrying lighted stars on top of poles as they sang to celebrate Epiphany.

A rather elaborate crèche from Traunkirchen was built by Josef Feichtinger and Josef Scheichl between the years 1890 and 1913. It was presented to the museum with the aid of the Salzburg Christmas Crèche Society, founded in 1916. An especially charming paper crèche from the Tirolean region was constructed around the beginning of the 19th century and donated to the Salzburg Museum by a local music society.

Their Relationship

The Salzburg Museum directors chose to display the crèche scenes with the Folk Toy Collection because of their latest research into the central meaning of the crèche itself. The crèche is in one respect as old as Christmas, but the earliest recorded use of the crèche is in the 13th century when St. Francis of Assisi used it to explain the Christmas story. Francis of Assisi gave us more than just the crèche scene, of course. He instilled in his followers an appreciation for the sacrosanct qualities of nature.

Accordingly, researchers for the Salzburg Museum believe that the crèche and its development over the years has perhaps never been more important to society than today. For, in the crèche, especially in the crèche scenes created in the Alpine regions, all of nature is brought into perspective. Today, when our natural environment is threatened by the industrialized world, it is more necessary than ever that we get back to the lessons of true environmentalism depicted so vividly in the crèche scenes of the Alpine people.

This concept of being in harmony with the environment brings us back to our opening theme. We all like

Market stall at street booth of local *Christkindlmarkt*.

to play! As one of the curators puts it, "There is none of the man in the child but there is a great deal of the child left in the grown man." We all like to play. To play is to fantasize, to create escape worlds where things are what we would like them to be. Investigating the ancient Christmas customs and practices of the people in the Salzburg region, scholars have discovered many folk traditions that can be described in no other way than as a form of play in which the nativity of Christ is at the heart of the play activity.

For example, farmers in the Salzburg area used to carry the figure of the pregnant Mary from farmstead to farmstead, hoping to find a place for her to stay. In like manner, the nuns in the Nonnberg Convent, located on a mountain in downtown Salzburg, continue a tradition on Christmas Eve. Each nun receives the opportunity to march up to the life-size crèche scene and rock the Christ figure in the crib for a few moments. Farmers in the vicinity of Salzburg are currently giving up the Christmas tree in favor of more crèche scenes. Downtown Salzburgers likewise no longer erect a large Christmas tree on the Old Market Square. Ever since 1970, a huge medallion-like crèche, the work of local father-son sculptors, Adlhart and Bernhard Prähauser, is erected on the square in place of the tree. Says Dr. Kutschera, "This is of

Rocking horse and horse and carriage with wax doll.

course merely play. On the other hand, this is also liturgy. Liturgy is both play and worship. It is leaving our prosaic world to spend a few moments in God's world. That is precisely what happens in play. Play, like liturgy, is an escape from our world into a world of the blessed."

In the mind's eye, then, play transforms the ordinary world of lifeless objects into a supernatural world alive with figures from heaven. Into these self-created figures, our imaginations breathe minds and souls. When we make crèches, we are not just depicting the nativity scene. In a real sense, we are engaging in play —in an act of creation. In this view, there reigns a total sense of unison and harmony. The harmony which the Alpine crèche-makers thus create between heaven, man, and nature should force us to take another serious look at what our new awareness of the environment can and should mean to mankind: an interaction between God, man, and the world for the good of all existence.

Conceived with this perspective, the Salzburgers think they have evolved a correct definition of human beings. They reject any view which defines people as determined by principles of behaviorism. Rather, they see them as defined and determined by the accumulative cultural structure of their environment. Custom and tradition are not only formative of men and women. Traditions and customs are also devices by which people solve problems. Accordingly, for example, we cannot speak of being conditioned for or against war; rather, aggression and fear can be controlled and channeled by the ritualized techniques of play. Since play and ritual are essentially the same,

we can view the individual differences and competitions between the peoples of each community in the Salzburg countryside as models of aggression and competition between nations. As each community of individuals expresses and copes with its aggressions through ritualistic devices—for example, crèche building, native costume competitions, and similar folkloric practices—so too other peoples of the world might learn to sublimate their differences through play and ritual.

Anthropologists too have recently been studying the Salzburg crèche scenes for what can be learned about this people's habits of interaction with their environment at the various times the crèches were built. Of special interest are the tools carried and used by the shepherd farmers in a few of the crèche scenes. For instance, shepherds in Salzburg and Tirolean crèches always carry a long pole at the end of which is attached a shovel-like blade. For years experts puzzled over the purpose of this tool. Now they have concluded that it was used only in areas where wolves were a constant threat to domestic animals. The long-handled tool was, in effect, a cupping device to scoop up stones and fling them at attacking predators with better than sling shot accuracy.

There is a great deal to be learned from the Christmas crèche. Recent insights reveal that the crèche, like play, tradition, and custom, cannot be segregated from human life itself. Far from being merely a representation of the Christmas story, the crèche is a cultural hand-me-down, which reveals the true values and life-styles of the people of their time.

Toy schoolroom.

Remembered Joy

The year is pierced
with remembered joy.
Snow falls heavily and
crusts the etchings of trees
and crinkles beneath boots.
"Lo, how a Rose" chimes memories
of hopes and beliefs sometimes
lost: that a Child is the
plumb line; that a birth's
miracle is not lost
in the years nor the centuries
nor the backaches nor the tears;
that Christmas balls slowly turning to the light,
evergreen scents, sliding snowy squeals,
and the treasured Infant
are the essence for us all.

CAROL HAMILTON

"Cover Him, Joseph"

"Cover him, Joseph, the evening is cold,
Night mists have fallen, the day has grown old;
Tired the people who toss in their sleep,
Weary the shepherds still watching their sheep."
    Tender the mother, gracious and mild,
    God in his mercy has given this child.

"Cover him, Joseph, the morning is bright,
Red clouds of dawn have taken their flight,
Sullen the heat of the day nearing noon,
This child so precious will grow up too soon."
    Thoughtful the mother, growing the boy,
    God in his mercy has given her joy.

"Cover him, Joseph, he's still a wee boy,
Hope binds us daily to heavenly joy;
Far in the future some dark days may loom—
Strengthen his life for those moments of gloom."
    Gentle the mother, gracious and fair,
    God in his mercy will answer her prayer.

WILSON C. EGBERT

Symbol

All I wish for Christmas
is one tree ornament
reminding me
of you.

One shiny ball
round as the earth
reflecting candlelight
perfectly formed
as only The Creation can be
having no beginning
and no end.
Reminding me.

VIVIAN M. LOKEN

Poems of Christmas

And Gabriel Said To Mary

"You may have the Son of man
for a space of borrowed years.
Only let him play;
let him be a child.

"Let him be the rebuke in temple tones,
the laughter in wedding bells.
Let him sing:
a winter's wail,
the allegro of spring,
the joy of dawn unto day.

"Let the swaddle-bands give way
to a seamless robe,
and the robe to sky.

"Untie the knotted ends of apron strings
and send him to all-brother,
all-sister, all-mother, all-father and God.

"But for now, rejoice
to the sound of new life in your womb,
to the smile of angels,
till God is born!"

MAYNARD E. STOKKA

Volume I - 1931

Volume II - 1932

Volume III - 1933

Volume IV - 1934

Volume V - 1935

Volume VI - 1936

Volume VII - 1937

Volume VIII - 1938

Volume IX - 1939

Volume X - 1940

Volume XI - 1941

Volume XII - 1942

Volume XIII - 1943

Volume XIV - 1944

CHRISTMAS 1977 is the 47th volume of the annual edited by its founder, Randolph E. Haugan. Through words, scenes, and melodies we celebrate anew the great festival of Christmas, in our own land and throughout the world, as we are given a fresh interpretation of the birth of Jesus. The type is set in Linotype Caledonia. Headings are set in Monotype Goudy Blackletter with Lombardic initials. *Christmas* is printed by photo-offset lithography and published by Augsburg Publishing House, Minneapolis, Minnesota.

Volume XV - 1945

Volume XVI - 1946

Volume XVII - 1947

Volume XVIII - 1948

Volume XIX - 1949

Volume XX - 1950

Volume XXI - 1951

Volume XXII - 1952

Volume XXIII - 1953

Volume XXIV - 1954

Volume XXV - 1955

Volume XXVI -1956

Volume XXVII - 1957

Volume XXVIII - 1958

Volume XXIX - 1959

Volume XXX - 1960

Volume XXXI - 1961

Volume XXXII - 1962

Volume XXXIII - 1963

Volume XXXIV - 1964

Volume XXXV - 1965

Volume XXXVI - 1966

Volume XXXVII - 1967

Volume XXXVIII - 1968

Volume XXXIX - 1969

Volume XL - 1970

Volume XLI - 1971

Volume XLII - 1972

Volume XLIII - 1973

Volume XLIV - 1974

Volume XLV - 1975

Volume XLVI - 1976